Applied Innovation and Technology Management

Series Editors

Technology is not just limited to technology companies. Managing innovation and technology is no longer a luxury and needs to be understood by all sectors around the world and by both technical and non-technical managers. This book series explores existing and emerging technologies that address current challenges within innovation and technology managements. Each title is developed to provide a set of frameworks, tools and methods that can be adopted by researchers, managers and student in engineering, innovation and technology fields. Research, policy and practice-based books in the series cover topics such as roadmapping, portfolio management, technology forecasting, R&D management, health technologies, bio technologies, transportation management, smart cities, and open innovation, among many others.

Jianxi Luo

Design Science

Driving Innovation with Unified Principles

Springer

Jianxi Luo
Department of Systems Engineering
City University of Hong Kong
Kowloon Tong, Hong Kong

ISSN 2662-9402 ISSN 2662-9410 (electronic)
Applied Innovation and Technology Management
ISBN 978-3-032-13352-6 ISBN 978-3-032-13353-3 (eBook)
https://doi.org/10.1007/978-3-032-13353-3

This Springer imprint is published by the registered company Springer Nature Switzerland AG
The registered company address is: Gewerbestrasse 11, 6330 Cham, Switzerland

Preface

Design, at its best, is disciplined imagination. It asks us to structure ambiguity, turn knowledge into form, and move ideas from possibility to reality—responsibly. This book, *Design Science: Driving Innovation with Unified Principles*, makes that discipline explicit. It treats design not as folklore or a bag of tricks, but as a science of creating the artificial: principled enough to teach and test, flexible enough to adapt, and human enough to matter.

Over two decades of practice, research, and education in design and innovation, I have witnessed design theories and methods proliferate and fragment: design thinking workshops on one side, engineering ontologies on another, entrepreneurship playbooks on a third—each useful, each partial. I have also seen the disconnect between unguided design practice and the existence of many design principles that can drive innovation. The central motivation of this book is integration.

I present and employ a unifying lens that views design as a system of Artifacts, Actions, and Actors (the 3A framework). It clarifies what is being shaped, how it is being shaped, and by whom. Across the book, 3A helps connect foundations (ontology, process, creativity, empathy) with practice (prototyping, flexibility, convergence), with complexity (architecture, change propagation), with AI (both AI for Design and Design for AI), and with outcomes that extend beyond the product—Design for X: business, entrepreneurship, public policy, and sustainability.

Two convictions run through the chapters that follow. First, innovation is rhythmic: effective efforts cycle between divergence and convergence—expanding options and then tightening with evidence and judgment. This cadence recurs across models and scales. Second, AI both shifts the feasible set and tightens the loop. Generative and agentic AI widen search and generation, accelerate convergence, and shorten iteration cycles. The gains arrive only when humans set goals, roles, guardrails, and escalation paths that keep hybrid intelligence reliable, contestable, and accountable.

This book is written for multiple audiences. Students and educators will find a clear spine of principles and methods—backed by figures, tables, and examples—that travels across domains and course formats. Practitioners and leaders will discover actionable strategies and tools for architecting products, processes, organizations, and AI-assisted workflows, with checklists, trade-off cues, and governance prompts to keep evidence and accountability in the loop. Researchers will meet an integrating language that links classic design theories to today's open questions at the AI–design frontier, pointing to testable hypotheses and promising seams for future work.

Here's the roadmap. The chapters form a coherent spine—from first principles to practice, from making to managing complexity, from human judgment to hybrid intelligence, and finally to outcomes and futures. Read straight through or enter vertically: take a principle, pair it with a method, and apply it in context. Recurring threads—divergence/convergence, ontology as language, prototyping as evidence, and AI as material and partner—bind the parts into a single practice. What follows is that spine:

- Chapters 1–2 (Foundations and Innovation). What design is, what design science contributes, and why design is the hinge between science and entrepreneurship.
- Chapters 3–4 (Process and Ontology). How processes make ambiguity discussable; how ontologies (FBS, Axiomatic Design, C-K, TRIZ, and more) make reasoning explicit and computable.
- Chapters 5, 6, and 7 (Creativity, Empathy, Heuristics). Creativity as transformation of knowledge; empathy from user- to humanity-centered; heuristics as the adaptable "toolbox" for action under uncertainty.
- Chapter 8 (Prototyping). Prototyping as thinking-through-making—where craft meets evidence and ideas earn their reality.
- Chapter 9–10 (Flexibility and Convergence). Designing options and architectures that can change; then deciding with discipline—verification, traceability, and commitments that hold in the world.
- Chapter 11 (Complexity). Structure governs behavior. We use design structure matrix (DSM) and change-propagation logic to see dependencies, localize risk, and steer emergence.
- Chapter 12 (Design and AI). AI as material and partner: ground, test, and govern to convert algorithmic capability into dependable capability—and design AI systems that deserve trust.
- Chapter 13 (Design for X). Beyond the artifact to outcomes: business models, ventures, policy instruments, and sustainability across the life cycle.
- Chapter 14 (Designing the Future). Return to 3A with a systemic, evolutionary stance: artifacts as evolvable architectures, actors as human–AI constellations with participation and power designed in, actions as instrumented, auditable, iterated interventions.

My hope is simple: that this book helps you design better things—and better consequences—faster and more reliably, with a shared language that lets diverse teams think together. Design transforms knowledge into action and artifacts; design science equips us, as actors, to do it better.

Kowloon Tong, Hong Kong Jianxi Luo

Acknowledgments

I am grateful to the many people who shaped my thinking about design science and innovation. Their work, collaborations, and conversations gave this book its contours and momentum—far more than a list can capture.

My first thanks are to my thesis advisors and professors who inspired me during my MIT years (2004–2010): Daniel Roos, Christopher Magee, Daniel Whitney, Carliss Baldwin, Joe Moses, James Utterback, and Olivier de Weck. Their guidance and encouragement formed my early habits of rigor and curiosity in design and systems thinking. I learned as much beyond MIT as within it. Through visits, seminars, and sustained discussions with John Paul McDuffie, Takahiro Fujimoto, Margaret Dalziel, Ki-Chan Kim, John Moavenzadeh, and Daniel Heller, I came to see more clearly how design operates inside firms and industries, in policy settings, and across global value chains. They broadened my field of view.

During my years at the Singapore University of Technology and Design (2012–2023)—conceived and built in collaboration with MIT—I honed my views on design science. I had the rare privilege of helping design a design university, shaping programs, studios, and research agendas where design served as the connective tissue across disciplines. Alongside building this ecosystem and culture, I became intent on laying a theoretical foundation for design education. I taught graduate courses in Design Science and undergraduate courses in design, innovation, and entrepreneurship, while supervising hundreds of student design projects from idea to pilot. In parallel, I pursued design science research—studying processes, artifacts, and designers—and translated those insights into design support tools to strengthen project-based learning. Anchored by the SUTD–MIT International Design Centre—whose ethos fused research, education, and practice—our classrooms and studios became living testbeds where the principles in this book were stress-tested, clarified, and made teachable.

This journey would not have been possible without the shared vision and sustained effort of my SUTD colleagues—drawn from many countries and disciplines—to build a design-driven, innovative university from the ground up: Thomas Magnanti, Kristin Wood, Aditya Mathur, Saif Benjaafar, Jeffrey Huang, Kevin Otto, Katja Hölttä-Otto, Ricardo Sosa, Martin Dunn, Lucienne Blessing, David Rosen,

Peter Jackson, Corinna Choong, Hong Yee Low, Rong Zhao, Arlindo Silva, Mohan Rajesh, Stylianos Dritsas, Sawako Kaijima, Chau Yuen, Belinda Yuen, Shaoying Huang, Michinao Hashimoto, Subburaj Karupppasamy, Suranga Nanayakkara, and Sayjel Patel, among others. Their collegiality—and their conviction that design can and should move education, research, and practice toward a better future—motivated and sustained this work.

My thinking has also been enriched by a wider community of co-authors, collaborators, and academic friends in design, creativity, and innovation: Panos Papalambros, John Gero, Alice Agogino, Maria Yang, Yongqi Lou, Peter Childs, Yoram Reich, Pascal Le Masson, Yukari Nagai, Roger Jiao, Yan Wang, Gaetano Cascini, Amresh Chakrabarti, Jason Woodard, Richard Buchanan, Don Norman, Tugrul Daim, Seng Beng Ho, Victor Tang, Min Xie, Ying Liu, Zhinan Zhang, Zhiyuan Cheng, Lan Xue, Katherine Morton, Li Zheng, Jizhen Li, Wei Zhang, Steven White, Ji Han, Babak Heydari, Christopher Mccomb, Kosa Goucher-Lambert, Faez Ahmed, Filippo Chiarello, Liuqing Chen, and Olga Kokshagina, among others. Their insights, critiques, and support enriched and sharpened this work.

Finally, this book reflects the energy and talent of researchers who worked with me as postdoctoral fellows and graduate students—many now faculty members and industry leaders: Bowen Yan, Jeffrey Alstott, Giorgio Triulzi, Srinivasan Venkataraman, Chaoyang Song, Diana Moreno, Bradley Camburn, Carlye Lauff, Binyang Song, Yuejun He, Serhad Sarica, Siddharth Lakshmi, Qihao Zhu, Shuo Jiang, and Patrick Karekezi. Their contributions and insights are evident on these pages. I also thank Ping Luo for assistance with many figures in this book.

Contents

Chapter 1
Design Science: What Is It

Abstract This chapter defines design as the intentional transformation of knowledge into novel, useful artifacts and argues for a science of design that makes practice teachable, auditable, and improvable. Tracing key foundations and the emergence of Design Science as a field, it introduces the Artifacts–Actions–Actors (3A) framework as a unifying lens. We position design science as a metascience for innovation, advancing unified principles that shift innovation from episodic luck to disciplined, repeatable progress across domains and scales.

What Is Design?

"Design" carries different meanings across contexts, but it always spans both process and outcome. As a verb, it denotes the deliberate effort to shape possibilities into form—to invent, adapt, and refine. As a noun, it names the results of that effort—the artifacts we create, tangible and intangible: products and software, services and organizations, policies and institutions. In short, design is the dynamic interplay between creating and what is created. For clarity in this book, I adopt a compact definition:

> Design is the intentional human endeavor that applies knowledge to create artifacts that are both novel and useful, with the aim of improving life.

At its core, design is a sophisticated human endeavor: it applies knowledge, couples it with imagination, and employs systematic problem-solving to produce novel, useful artifacts. These artifacts range from humble tools to complex socio-technical systems, reshaping environments, economies, and daily life. In our era, civilization is defined less by what we discover in nature than by what we design.

Unlike natural evolution—which proceeds blindly and slowly—design is purposeful: it looks ahead, weighs time and cost, and steers toward preferred futures (Dennett, 2015). Humans are distinctive in the scale and speed of this intentional shaping: we design technologies, markets, institutions, and infrastructures,

J. Luo, *Design Science*, Applied Innovation and Technology Management,
https://doi.org/10.1007/978-3-032-13353-3_1

harnessing knowledge, imagination, and tools to make better futures by design rather than by accident.

The result is a hybrid world in which designed and evolved systems coexist, with selection pressures continuing to favor some configurations over others (Arthur, 2009). Our daily lives run on designed—yet continually evolving—infrastructure for food and energy, transportation and logistics, communications and finance, all interlocking with natural ecosystems (de Weck et al., 2011). Artificial intelligence (AI) now joins this landscape as a deliberately designed layer of cognition, extending human capability while introducing new risks and responsibilities.

As these artificial constructs grow in reach and consequence, so too does the imperative to understand—and continually improve—our capacity to design. This calls for a clearer science of design, with shared principles, methods, representations, and languages that render practice teachable, auditable, and improvable.

What Is Design Science?

Design science may be characterized as a systematic, theory-informed inquiry into the processes, representations, and decisions by which novel, useful artifacts are produced—and into the means by which those processes can be rendered teachable, auditable, and improvable across domains. Rather than displacing disciplinary design practices (e.g., in engineering, architecture, business, or government), design science seeks the shared abstractions and methods that allow insights to travel among them.

The concept has matured through successive clarifications. Sydney Gregory (1966) argued that, although design is not a natural science, it contains scientific aspects amenable to disciplined analysis—especially in its methods and problem-structuring practices—thus moving debate beyond anecdote toward methodology. Buckminster Fuller (1969) popularized "design science" as the purposive, systematic application of scientific insight to improve human conditions, recasting design as a lever for societal and sustainability challenges.

A decisive theoretical move came with Herbert Simon's *The Sciences of the Artificial* (1969), which distinguished the descriptive aims of natural science (what is) from the normative ambitions of design (what ought to be). Simon's framing legitimized scientific study of the artificial—organizations, products, policies, and other designed systems. Subsequent work deepened this stance. Nigel Cross (2001) articulated "designerly ways of knowing," identifying cognitive styles and representational forms distinctive to design yet complementary to scientific and artistic inquiry. Youbai Xie (2014) treated design as a knowledge-driven, evolving, and competitive activity amenable to analysis and improvement, emphasizing general principles and methods that link objectives, constraints, knowledge, and process.

Institutionally, the establishment of the journal *Design Science*, co-founded by Panos Papalambros and John Gero, consolidated the field's scope as the rigorous study of artifacts and systems embedded within physical, psychological, economic,

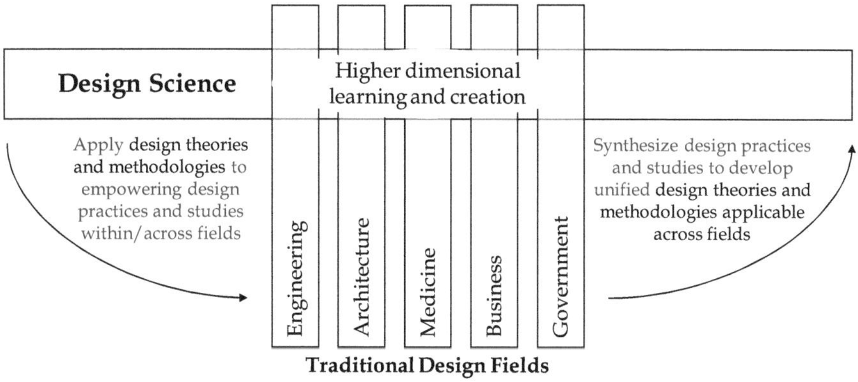

Fig. 1.1 Design science as a metascience (Luo, 2025)

social, and virtual environments, and of the interplay between analysis and synthesis in advancing products and systems across disciplines (Papalambros, 2015; Papalambros et al., 2025). This consolidation underscored the field's transdisciplinary posture and its commitment to a unified inquiry that crosses disciplinary boundaries.

In sum, design science is a transdisciplinary field that synthesizes insights from engineering, architecture, medicine, business, public policy, and other domains. It investigates how designing is performed through (i) explanatory accounts—how problems are framed, alternatives generated and represented, choices made, and solutions realized—and (ii) prescriptive instruments—principles, methods, and computational supports—that improve those activities in practice. Crucially, its findings feed back into specialized domains to drive innovation, productivity, and societal progress (Fig. 1.1).

Accordingly, design science is best understood as a *metascience*: a unifying inquiry that draws upon diverse, specialized practices through shared languages, methods, and logics, cultivating a holistic understanding of design across contexts. In brief, this book adopts the following working definition:

> Design science is the systematic, transdisciplinary study of how human actors create novel and useful artifacts through interconnected and often experimental actions, with the goal of understanding and improving design across domains. Design science is a metascience.

A Unifying Lens for Design Science: Artifacts, Actions, and Actors (3A)

In this book, the Artifacts–Actions–Actors (3A) framework is introduced as a systematic lens for making design legible, testable, and comparable across domains (Fig. 1.2). It distinguishes three coupled elements of design: what is being shaped (artifacts), who participates and with what capacities (actors), and how work proceeds (actions). Using 3A, we can map hypotheses to prototypes, roles to

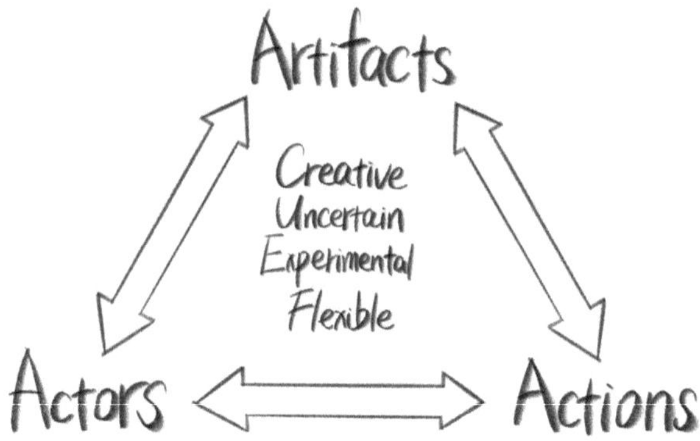

Fig. 1.2 The Artifact-Action-Actor (3A) framework for design science (Luo, 2025)

responsibilities, and outcomes to evidence across scales (component → system → ecosystem) and time horizons (now → next → beyond). We will use 3A throughout as a common language for analyzing design.

Artifacts denote the full range of human creations—from material objects, machines, software, products, and buildings to services, organizations, and complex socio-technical systems (e.g., business models, public policies, social protocols, and infrastructures). Following Buchanan (2001), designed artifacts can be viewed along four increasing orders of complexity.

- First order: symbols, graphics, and visual communications
- Second order: tangible products encompassing form, function, and usability
- Third order: interactive experiences, services, and human-machine interactions over time
- Fourth order: systems of systems, such as organizational structures, governance, urban, ecological, and global infrastructures

Actions encompass the processes and methodologies by which designing unfolds—including methods and heuristics, representations, experiments, governance practices, and the sequence of decisions over time that moves work from possibility to commitment. Representation choices shape what is perceived, heuristics steer exploration, experiments generate evidence, governance sets guardrails, and decision sequences pace convergence. Recurring action families—empathizing, ideating, prototyping, testing, evaluating—are rarely sequential; they are iterative, coupled, and interdependent. This dynamic interplay is the lived texture of design.

Actors include individuals, teams, organizations, ecosystems, and even nations that drive or participate in design. Their scale and complexity vary widely—from solitary inventors (e.g., Thomas Edison) and breakthrough teams (e.g., Bell Labs' transistor group), to corporations (e.g., OpenAI), national programs (e.g., NASA), and increasingly, AI agents. Creativity is central to understanding actors and is shaped by interdependent forces across levels: individual cognition and disposition, group dynamics, organizational culture, and the broader institutional and societal environment.

Design science addresses not only these three pillars—artifacts, actions, and actors—but also their dynamic interplay. Because design seeks to create the new, all three are shot through with uncertainty. This makes experimentation essential: actions should be structured as tests, actors must embrace trial and error, and artifacts should remain flexible—easy to vary, instrument, and iterate at low cost and high speed. Under such conditions, artifacts, actions, and actors co-evolve, each reshaping the others as evidence accumulates (Luo, 2010).

Design Science: A Metascience for Innovation

Design is the hinge of innovation: it translates knowledge into testable propositions, manufacturable forms, viable services, and governable systems. Sitting at the intersection of science (discovering how the world works) and entrepreneurship (organizing value creation and diffusion)—design makes ideas buildable and scalable. Studying that translation scientifically—how ideas are framed, represented, evaluated, and realized—turns innovation from episodic luck into disciplined progress.

Unified principles make that progress repeatable. A science of design contributes shared ontologies and representations to make reasoning explicit; process models that render ambiguity discussable; fast-and-frugal heuristics for acting under uncertainty; computational support for simulation and AI-assisted reasoning; and evidence-anchored governance to keep traceability and accountability in the loop. Effective efforts work to a rhythm: diverge to expand options and surface hidden constraints; converge to choose, verify, and move.

Taken together, these principles—ontology, process discipline, heuristics, computation, and governance—constitute a coherent toolkit that widens search without getting lost and tightens decisions without becoming brittle. Anchored by the 3A framework (Artifacts–Actions–Actors), they ground a shared theory-and-method set that travels across domains, elevating creativity while keeping evidence in the loop. In short, they equip designers to navigate—and shape—innovation in an increasingly designed, complex world.

References

Arthur, W. B. (2009). *The nature of technology: What it is and how it evolves*. Free Press (Simon & Schuster).

Buchanan, R. (2001). Design research and the new learning. *Design Issues, 17*(4), 3–23.

Cross, N. (2001). Designerly ways of knowing: Design discipline versus design science. *Design Issues, 17*(3), 49–55.

de Weck, O. L., Roos, D., & Magee, C. L. (2011). *Engineering systems: Meeting human needs in a complex technological world*. MIT Press.

Dennett, D. (2015). *Information, evolution, and intelligent design*. Seminar at Royal Institution.

Fuller, R. B. (1969). *Utopia or oblivion: The prospects for humanity*. Penguin Books.

Gregory, S. A. (1966). *The design method*. Butterworths.
Luo, J. (2010). *Hierarchy in industry architecture: Transaction strategy under technological constraints* [Ph.D. thesis, Massachusetts Institute of Technology, Cambridge, MA, United States].
Luo, J. (2025). Design science: What is it? In *3rd IEEE International Conference on Design Science*, Shanghai, China.
Papalambros, P. Y. (2015). Design science: Why, what and how. *Design Science, 1*, e1.
Papalambros, P. Y., Gero, J. S., Maier, A. M., Cagan, J., Ahmed-Kristensen, S., Albers, A., April, L., Blessing, L., Boujut, J.-F., Cantamessa, M., Cascini, G., Chakrabarti, A., Chen, C.-H., Clarkson, P. J., Eckert, C., Feinberg, F., Gericke, K., Hanna, S., Holtta-Otto, K., Jankovic, M., Jin, Y., Kleinsmann, M., Knight, P., Le Masson, P., Lewis, K., Linsey, J., Luo, J., McMahon, C., Nagai, Y., Pigosso, D. C. A., Reich, Y., Reid, T., Seepersad, C. C., Seifert, C. M., Shealy, T., Summers, J. D., Tripp, J., Vermaas, P. E., Wartzack, S., Yang, M. C., & Yannou, B. (2025). Design science: Why, what and how – Revisited. *Design Science, 11*, e48.
Simon, H. A. (1969). *The sciences of the artificial*. MIT Press.
Xie, Y. (2014). Four basic laws in design science. *China Engineering Science, 2*(12), 2–9.

Chapter 2
Design for Innovation

Abstract Innovation sits at the intersection of science, design, and entrepreneurship. This chapter articulates the United Innovation Process, showing how design translates scientific insight into testable inventions and prepares them for entrepreneurial scaling. Through selected cases and programs that illustrate integration at the individual, organizational, and ecosystem levels, we offer guidance on aligning incentives and value creation across actions spanning science, design, and entrepreneurship—to strengthen innovation outcomes.

How Innovation Comes

More than a century ago, economist Joseph Schumpeter argued that long-run growth depends on innovation as *creative destruction*—the continual displacement of the old by the new through entrepreneurial action (Schumpeter, 1934). Robert Solow later quantified this insight, demonstrating that over 80% of U.S. economic growth in the first half of the twentieth century stemmed from technological progress rather than increases in labor or capital (Solow, 1957). Innovation is not merely an economic abstraction—it is a human imperative. It underpins our ability to tackle climate change, improve public health, and sustain global prosperity.

While innovation is often championed as the goal, far less attention is paid to the process that leads to it. Our understanding of how innovation happens, and how best to enable it, remains fragmented. Innovation requires a confluence of new discoveries in science, technological inventions, and entrepreneurial action. However, we struggle to turn discoveries into inventions and transform inventions into innovations that deliver significant economic and societal impact.

In *Science, the Endless Frontier* (1945), Vannevar Bush championed federal support for basic research with the promise of societal benefit, laying the foundation for a model in which scientific inquiry fuels real-world innovation. His vision helped institutionalize the idea that investment in fundamental science would naturally translate into technological progress and economic growth. Yet decades of experience have revealed that the "science → industry" pipeline is far more complex than

J. Luo, *Design Science*, Applied Innovation and Technology Management,
https://doi.org/10.1007/978-3-032-13353-3_2

initially imagined. New discoveries in science, while essential, do not automatically lead to innovation.

Political scientist Donald Stokes therefore proposed the concept of "use-inspired basic research"—curiosity-driven inquiry oriented toward practical goals—modeled on the work of biochemist Louis Pasteur. Today, agencies like DARPA and ARPA-H fund collaborative teams of scientists and engineers to pursue research grounded in real-world use cases, yielding breakthroughs ranging from GPS to speech recognition. Still, even use-inspired science does not guarantee innovation. The missing link is design, which applies knowledge to create artifacts that people can use.

Design serves as the critical translation engine that transforms abstract scientific knowledge into tangible, useful technologies, systems, and services. It bridges the gap between theoretical insight and practical application, giving form and function to ideas that might otherwise remain dormant. With design, discoveries acquire the shape, usability, and relevance needed to become inventions. Yet invention, while essential, is only a step on the path to innovation. True innovation requires not just novelty, but adoption, scalability, and sustained impact in the real world.

As Singapore's founding father Lee Kuan Yew aptly emphasized: "The economy is driven by new knowledge, new discoveries in science and technology, innovations that are taken to market by entrepreneurship." Innovation happens when inventions reach users and markets, creating real-world impact. Entrepreneurship is therefore the driving catalyst in this process—mobilizing resources, navigating uncertainty, and unlocking value. Yet even the most visionary entrepreneur needs something to work with. That "something" is the designed artifact: the tangible embodiment of scientific insight, shaped for usability, desirability, and relevance.

Entrepreneurship can itself be seen as a sophisticated act of systems design. Entrepreneurs must not only create new products and services, but also architect the organizations, processes, and business models that bring these offerings to users. This involves designing pathways for delivery, mechanisms for growth, and structures that generate value across a diverse range of stakeholders—from customers and employees to investors and society at large.

Therefore, bridging the gap between scientific discoveries and usable innovation requires complementary efforts of design and entrepreneurship. Design applies knowledge creatively to invent novel and useful artifacts—products, systems, and services that embody scientific insight in accessible and functional forms. Entrepreneurship then propels these artifacts into the world, delivering them to markets, users, and ecosystems where they can generate real value. In this dynamic interplay, design serves as the vital connector between science and entrepreneurship, translating abstract ideas into tangible opportunities.

Science, Design, and Entrepreneurship

Each activity plays a distinct role: science, driven by curiosity, uncovers new truths and expands knowledge; design, fueled by creativity and knowledge, invents novel artifacts; and entrepreneurship, focused on value, propels those inventions into the world, turning them into impactful innovations.

- Science seeks truth and produces discoveries.
- Design seeks possibility and produces inventions.
- Entrepreneurship seeks value and produces innovations.

These activities often remain fragmented because the people who perform them differ in goals and culture: scientists driven by curiosity probe the unknown; designers translate insights into usable and meaningful solutions; and entrepreneurs marshal resources and accept risk to bring those solutions to market.

- Scientists seek to discover truths about the world.
- Designers strive to create novel and useful artifacts.
- Entrepreneurs aim to realize value via implementation and scale.

Scientists, designers, and entrepreneurs operate under different incentives, methods, and professional languages, leaving the three pillars of innovation in separate silos. As a result, discoveries often languish in academic journals, designs lack cutting-edge insight, and entrepreneurs have no differentiated product to scale—squandering investment and opportunity. Transformative breakthroughs emerge only when science, design, and entrepreneurship interact dynamically, making an integrated framework that unites these activities indispensable.

The United Innovation Process

To bridge these silos, I proposed the *United Innovation Process* (Luo, 2015)—an action-based framework that treats innovation as the dynamic coupling of three sub-processes. Science generates discoveries about how the world works. Design translates this knowledge into novel, useful inventions. Entrepreneurship scales those inventions into widespread, value-creating innovations. Crucially, design sits at the center of the triad, acting as the translation engine that converts abstract scientific insight into artifacts ready for entrepreneurial delivery and societal impact (Fig. 2.1).

Uniting science, design, and entrepreneurship benefits all parties:

- For science, integration enhances real-world relevance and brings impact. It guides scientific iniquity toward solving real-world problems of societal significance, enables faster translation of findings, and accelerates funding from downstream entrepreneurial commercialization.
- For design, integration enriches the creative process with scientific insight, enhances creativity through the access and use of scientific and cutting-edge

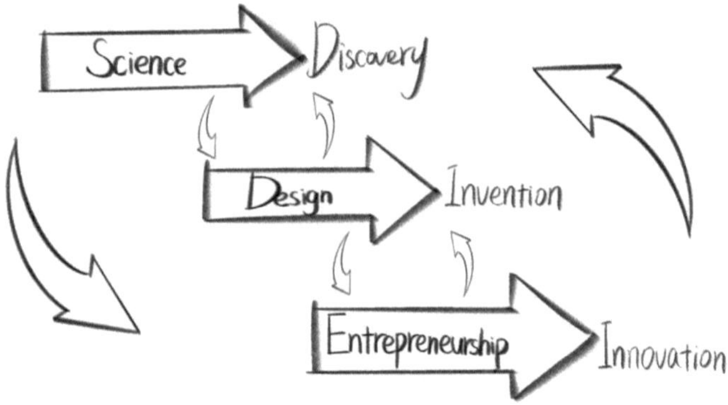

Fig. 2.1 The United Innovation Process (Luo, 2015)

knowledge, aligns with societal needs and downstream feasibility, and increases the likelihood of breakthrough inventions.

- For entrepreneurship, it offers first-mover advantage, differentiation through novel products based on cutting-edge science, and more sustainable business models based on deep science.

Together, this triad enhances the likelihood of radical, frequent, and high-impact innovations. The most dynamic innovation ecosystems—Silicon Valley, Israel, MIT, Stanford—are living examples of this integration in action. When design, science, and entrepreneurship operate in concert rather than isolation, innovation accelerates. It becomes not only faster and bolder, but also more resilient and sustainable, capable of adapting to evolving challenges and delivering lasting value.

For example, the discovery of mRNA mechanisms in molecular biology could not have saved lives during the COVID-19 pandemic without the design of delivery systems, formulations, packaging, and vaccines. These designs, in turn, would have stayed in labs without the entrepreneurial efforts to test, produce, and distribute mRNA vaccines globally by companies like Moderna and BioNTech. Design made science usable; entrepreneurship made it impactful.

Design is the hinge of the United Innovation Process. It translates scientific discoveries into tangible inventions and readying those inventions for entrepreneurial scale-up. It links the curiosity-driven world of science with the opportunity-driven world of business: without design, discoveries remain abstract, entrepreneurs lack novel, human-centered offerings. Far from a linear hand-off, the three sub-processes form an iterative, mutually reinforcing ecosystem. Scientific insights spark fresh design possibilities; design challenges raise new research questions; and entrepreneurial feedback refines both science and design. In this dynamic interplay, design is the integrative, generative force that turns knowledge into value.

This framework also helps to distinguish three often-blurred concepts:

- Discovery (via science) is about understanding the unknown. It yields new knowledge and explanations about how the world works.

- Invention (via design) is about creating the new. It produces novel artifacts, processes, or experiences.
- Innovation (via entrepreneurship) is about achieving impact. It involves implementation, adoption, and value realization.

Design bridges discovery and invention, then readies invention for innovation. It gives form to ideas, translating abstract findings into testable, usable artifacts through iterative, human-centered experimentation. Entrepreneurs then mobilize resources and business models to scale these inventions into full-fledged innovations.

Science, design, and entrepreneurship are different, complementary activities. Meanwhile, they share three core characteristics.

- They are creative: They generate novel outputs—whether ideas, artifacts, or ventures.
- They are uncertain: The outcomes are not fully predictable; trial, error, and iteration are necessary.
- They are costly: They require resources—cognitive, temporal, and financial.

These shared traits suggest design is particularly suited to lead this integration of the triad because it naturally blends creativity with pragmatic problem-solving. It engages with uncertainty by prototyping and iterating. It enables learning through making. It creates forms that entrepreneurs can scale, and scientists can explore.

Integration Across Levels

Science, design, and entrepreneurship can be united in various ways across levels of individuals, organizations, and ecosystem. For example, Steve Wozniak, the co-founder of Apple, typified the designer driven by the joy of creation. Steve Jobs, by contrast, was a classic entrepreneur—motivated by societal impact and business success. The collaboration of Wozniak and Jobs at Apple demonstrates how integrating different roles can generate innovation. Wozniak brought technical ingenuity (science and design), while Jobs shaped the product vision and user experience and built the business (design and entrepreneurship).

In fact, integration need not be limited to teams—it can also reside within individuals. For example, Bob Langer at MIT embodies all three roles. As a prolific biomedical engineer, he publishes groundbreaking scientific research, designs advanced drug delivery systems, and co-founds startup companies to commercialize his work, bringing science-based inventions to patients and markets. He represents a united innovator—scientist, designer, and entrepreneur. Similarly, Demis Hassabis, co-founder and CEO of DeepMind, merges science, design, and entrepreneurship by developing AI models that solve scientific problems while advancing business goals. In 2024, Demis Hassabis and his colleague John Jumper were jointly awarded the Nobel Prize in Chemistry for their AI research contributions for protein structure prediction.

Organizations like Bell Labs and DeepMind, and ecosystems like Silicon Valley, institutionalize such integration. For example, Bell Labs institutionalized the United Innovation Process model by co-locating scientists, engineering designers, and business developers to invent impactful technologies like the transistor and laser. The invention of the transistor by Bardeen, Shockley, and Brattain at Bell Labs was deeply scientific but also designed with commercial implementation in mind—eventually catalyzing the digital revolution.

Silicon Valley and Shenzhen provide ecosystemic examples where integration of these activities fuels regional innovation leadership. Such innovative ecosystems thrive because they foster tight feedback loops between scientific inquiry, design experimentation, and entrepreneurial execution. But such ecosystems may take different paths to develop toward unifying the triad of science, design, and entrepreneurship. Silicon Valley grew from scientific and defense roots toward design and entrepreneurship. Shenzhen, by contrast, followed a reverse path—growing from commerce to manufacturing and then to design and now increasingly to science through new research universities establishment with government investment.

These cases illustrate that integration of science, design, and entrepreneurship can occur at multiple levels—within individuals, across organizations, or throughout regional ecosystems. Moreover, this integration may follow diverse evolutionary pathways, shaped by unique contexts, capabilities, and trajectories. Whether through personal initiative, institutional strategy, or ecosystem-wide collaboration, the convergence of these three activities consistently emerges as the critical driver of impactful innovation. Regardless of scale or structure, integration remains the key to unlocking sustained impact.

From Actor- to Action-Based View

Traditional models of innovation emphasize institutions—government, industry, and academia—and their integration. The United Innovation Process offers an alternative lens: an action-based view that highlights how the three actions—science, design, and entrepreneurship—interact to foster more radical, frequent, and impactful innovations, regardless of who performs them (Fig. 2.2).

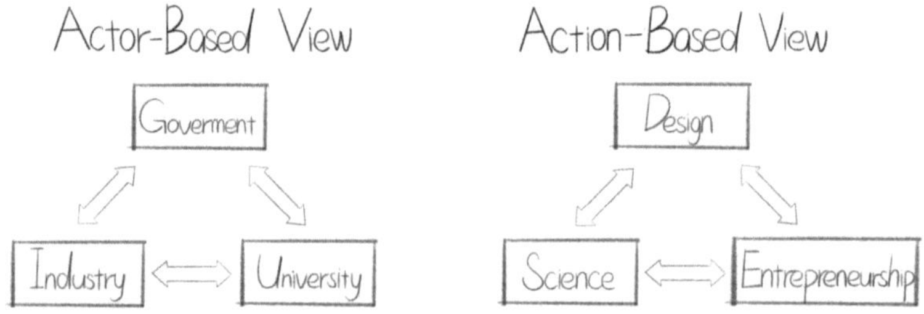

Fig. 2.2 The actor-based vs. action-based views of innovation ecosystems

This shift in perspective invites educators, policymakers, and leaders to cultivate environments that support integrated activity. Universities should teach not only science, entrepreneurship, or design but also the vital connections between them. Design education can play a key role in fostering such integration and synthesis. Companies should nurture interdisciplinary teams, while design-driven innovation projects can help form and bind these diverse groups. Governments, in turn, should fund programs that unite curiosity-driven research with design thinking and market potential.

Even when governments acknowledge the need for integration—through initiatives like the U.S. CHIPS and Science Act or agencies such as DARPA and ARPA-H—deep-rooted cultural and methodological barriers often persist. These efforts signal progress, but funding alone is not enough. What's truly needed is a shift in mindset: a new innovation model that unites science, design, and entrepreneurship into a cohesive, collaborative process. Only by reimagining how these disciplines interact can we unlock the full potential of transformative innovation.

Toward Design Science for Innovation

Recognizing design as the central integrator in the innovation process reinforces the importance of design science. We must move beyond treating design as an intuitive art and study it as a rigorous discipline—one that explains how knowledge is transformed into meaningful artifacts. Nor is it sufficient to study design in isolation. To maximize real world impact, we must examine how design operates at the intersection of scientific knowledge production and entrepreneurial value creation.

Design science offers theoretical frameworks, principles, and methods to explain how creativity works, how ideas take form, and how design decisions shape innovative outcomes. It provides enough structure to guide reasoning and practice under uncertainty while preserving room for exploration. In doing so, it makes the innovation process—as a whole—more effective, inclusive, and adaptable. This book takes up that challenge.

Having established design's central role in innovation, the chapters that follow explore the science of design—its foundations, core ontologies, unified principles, practical methods, and applications across domains. We show how disciplined design drives innovation. The aim is a coherent toolkit and shared language readers can adapt to their contexts—keeping exploration disciplined, collaboration aligned, and impact measurable.

> Design transforms knowledge into actions and artifacts. Design science equips us as actors to do it better.

References

Bush, V. (1945). *Science, the endless frontier: A report to the president on a program for postwar scientific research*. United States.

Luo, J. (2015). The united innovation process: Integrating science, design and entrepreneurship as sub-processes. *Design Science, 1*, e2.

Schumpeter, J. A. (1934). *The theory of economic development: An inquiry into profits, capital, credit, interest, and the business cycle*. Harvard University Press.

Solow, R. M. (1957). Technical change and the aggregate production function. *The Review of Economics and Statistics, 39*(3), 312–320.

Chapter 3
Design Process

Abstract Design rarely proceeds linearly. We compare human-centered models (IDEO, Double Diamond, d.school) with engineering and new product development (NPD) frameworks (Pahl & Beitz, V-model, Stage-Gate, Lean Startup), then situate AI-augmented cycles (Double Hump) that widen search and tighten evidence loops. The chapter equips readers to select and hybridize processes based on uncertainty and cost of late change, emphasizing cadence (divergence/convergence), accountability at gates, and the importance of process literacy over one-size-fits-all prescriptions.

Why Process Models Matter for Design

The United Innovation Process frames innovation as a triad in which design forges the vital bridge between science and entrepreneurship. Yet design itself is rarely linear; it meanders, loops, and sometimes doubles back. Process models give that design journey a map. They make ambiguity discussable, complexity navigable, and creativity manageable.

A clear model signals where to start, how to explore, when to converge, and where to pass the baton. Because those signals shape team roles, funding gates, and operating norms, process models are more than academic diagrams—they are innovation tools and pedagogical scaffolds. They influence team dynamics and resource allocation, and they can imprint organizational culture.

In what follows, we widen the lens from open-ended, empathy-driven design-thinking loops to the meticulously documented workflows of heavy engineering; from fast, data-rich, AI-assisted cycles to the heuristics of veteran designers who "feel" their way forward. Mastery comes not from memorizing a single canonical model, but from knowing several, reading context, and switching fluidly among them.

J. Luo, *Design Science*, Applied Innovation and Technology Management,
https://doi.org/10.1007/978-3-032-13353-3_3

Design-Thinking Models

Human-centered design-thinking models dominate innovation workshops because they travel well across domains and foreground empathy, creativity, and rapid iteration. They give non-specialist teams a shared language and cadence—without demanding deep technical tooling—so organizations can start doing design, not just talking about it. Below are three widely used patterns and what they are good for.

IDEO's three-phase model (Brown, 2008)—Inspiration → Ideation → Implementation—invites multidisciplinary teams to immerse in user contexts, diverge boldly, and prototype early. Its simplicity makes it a common backbone in social-innovation labs and MBA curricula; the risk is mistaking the phases for a strict sequence. Treat them as overlapping modes rather than gates.

- Inspiration—understand users, contexts, and constraints
- Ideation—generate, combine, and rough-test possibilities
- Implementation—pilot, iterate, and scale what works

The UK Design Council's Double Diamond (Fig. 3.1) adds structure by explicitly pairing divergence and convergence in two spaces—problem and solution. The model highlights four actions across the "diamonds" and helps teams balance creativity with focus; it is often adapted for public-sector innovation, service design, and policy work. Used well, it separates framing the right problem from building the right solution, encourages evidence at each gate, and normalizes looping between the diamonds when new findings reframe the brief.

- Discover—explore the problem space (diverge)
- Define—frame and select the problem (converge)
- Develop—explore the solution space (diverge)
- Deliver—select and refine the solution (converge)

The d.school's five-stage loop—Empathize, Define, Ideate, Prototype, Test (Stanford d.school, 2022)—puts "learning by making" at the center and normalizes *failing forward*. Novices value its clarity; experienced teams use it more fluidly, revisiting stages as evidence accumulates. The art lies in choosing inflection points: when to stop prototyping and move to pilot, when to loop back to Empathize after a surprising test (Fig. 3.2).

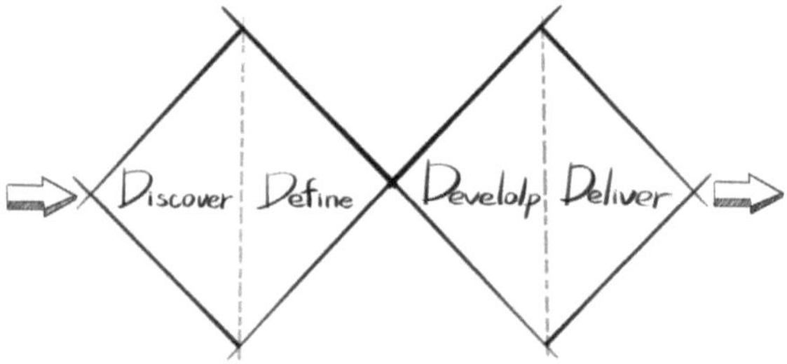

Fig. 3.1 The Double Diamond Process Model (UK Design Council)

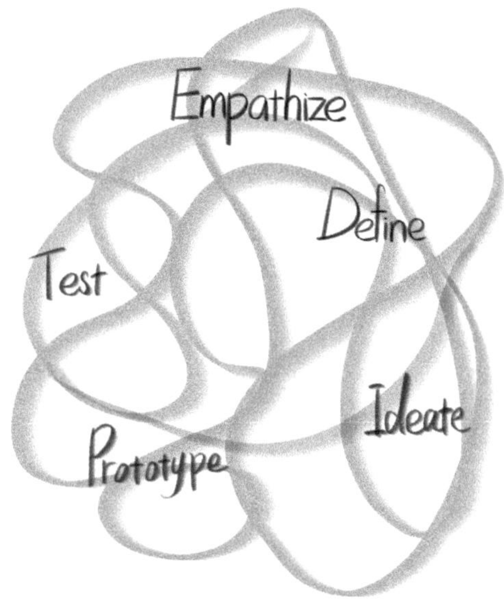

Fig. 3.2 The five key actions in design thinking

- Empathize—engage users to understand experiences and needs
- Define—synthesize insights into a sharp problem statement
- Ideate—create a broad set of candidate solutions
- Prototype—build quick, low-fidelity experiments
- Test—gather feedback, learn, and iterate

To use these models well, treat them as maps, not mandates. None is a waterfall. Teams should expect nonlinearity, iterate across stages, and calibrate the width of divergence and the criteria for convergence to context (risk, budget, evidence needs). As later sections show, these human-centered models may interoperate with more formal engineering workflows; the key is to select the right level of structure for the problem at hand and to keep learning loops short and accountable.

Engineering Design Models

The design-thinking models emphasize empathy, rapid frugal experimentation, and short iteration cycles. Adopted uncritically, they can underplay the rigor required for complex engineering or regulatory compliance. More structured models add systematic problem-solving, traceability, and risk control—non-negotiables in safety-critical domains such as medical devices and spacecraft.

Pahl and Beitz (2007) describe a four-phase flow—Planning, Concept, Embodiment, Detail (Fig. 3.3)—that mirrors systems-engineering logic: decompose problems, optimize subsystems, and reduce risk through structure. Each gate finalizes requirements, narrowing design freedom while increasing commitment. In

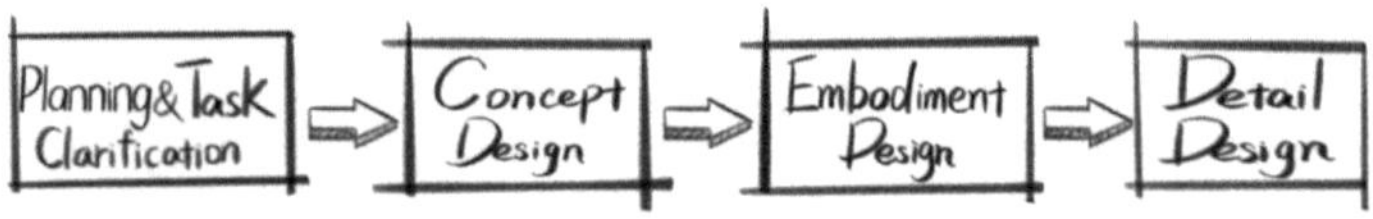

Fig. 3.3 Engineering Design Process Model (Pahl & Beitz, 2007)

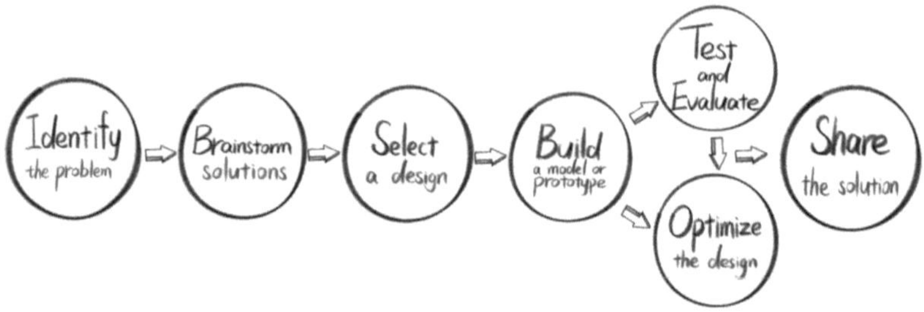

Fig. 3.4 NASA's Engineering Design Process Model

modern aerospace and automotive design programs, model-based systems engineering (MBSE) is commonly applied between Concept and Embodiment to support requirements flow-down, interface definition, and verification planning.

- Planning and task clarification—establish requirements, constraints, and success criteria
- Concept design—generate and compare high-level solution principles
- Embodiment design—develop architecture, form, functions, and interfaces
- Detail design—specify materials, dimensions, tolerances, and manufacturing processes

NASA's Engineering Design Process (Fig. 3.4) covers similar stages but places stronger emphasis on stakeholder alignment, constraints, teamwork, documentation, and verification/validation—essentials for aerospace and other mission-critical systems. In practice, it formalizes disciplined reviews, requirements traceability, and risk/hazard analysis to keep complexity and safety under control. Variants of this model are also widely used in STEM (Science, Technology, Engineering, and Mathematics) education to teach systematic process thinking, evidence-based iteration, and collaborative roles—habits that transfer well beyond engineering.

In addition, many defense contractors overlay the classic V-model—left branch for decomposition, right for integration—on Pahl and Beitz to align architecture, requirements, and verification (Forsberg et al., 2005). For software-intensive systems, the Spiral model—plan, risk, engineer, evaluate—supports iterative, risk-driven convergence while still meeting contract milestones (Boehm, 1988).

These Engineering Design Process models provide clear milestones, accountability, and traceability (e.g., requirements matrices, test plans, certification artifacts). Yet the same structure can introduce rigidity, slow feedback, and dampen creativity if followed dogmatically. Many organizations therefore hybridize—pairing V-model discipline with agile increments, human-centered discovery, and fast prototyping—to keep assurance high without sacrificing learning.

New Product Development Models

New product development (NPD) models in innovation management overlap with engineering design processes but extend them into market creation and commercialization. They structure the journey from opportunity identification and user insights to concept generation, validation, and launch—integrating design with market analysis, supply chain readiness, and manufacturing scale-up.

Ulrich and Eppinger's NPD flow aligns design milestones with marketing, operations, and manufacturing gates so that customer requirements, technical feasibility, and production constraints evolve in step (Ulrich & Eppinger, 2011). Cooper's Stage-Gate system operationalizes investment control: at each gate, sponsors review scope, risk, evidence, and expected return before releasing resources (Cooper, 1990). Together, these models emphasize cross-functional collaboration, explicit criteria at decision points, and early consideration of downstream constraints.

When the business model is as uncertain as the product, Lean Startup (Ries, 2011) substitutes long plans with an evidence loop—Build → Measure → Learn. The minimum viable product (MVP) trims effort to the smallest testable offer, puts it in front of early adopters, extracts validated learning, and guides a pivot or persevere decision. In this sense, Lean Startup functions as an NPD model for entrepreneurial contexts, prioritizing speed to signal, hypothesis testing, and capital efficiency (Fig. 3.5).

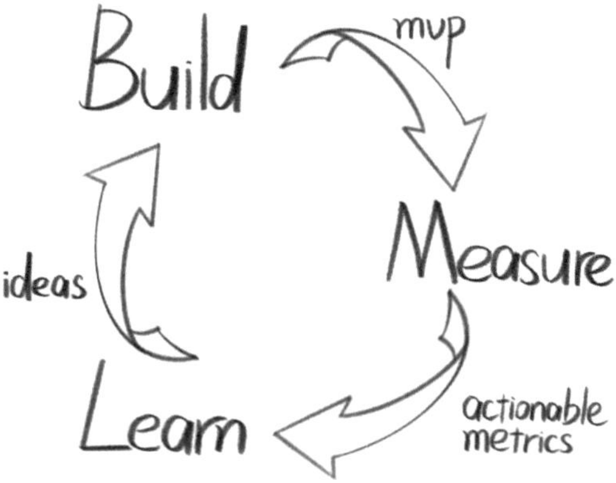

Fig. 3.5 Lean Startup Process Model (Ries, 2011)

AI-Augmented and Data-Driven Models

The Double Hump Model (Luo, 2023) elevates Opportunity Discovery/Evaluation and Design Generation/Evaluation into twin divergent–convergent cycles ("humps"). Higher humps indicate a process capable of surfacing more—and better—opportunities and producing more—and better—designs (Fig. 3.6). Modern machine-learning and generative pipelines supercharge both humps by widening search, accelerating iteration, and tightening evidence feedback.

In practice, the model pairs generative algorithms with human judgment to enlarge both the opportunity and design spaces while keeping decisions accountable. Data pipelines—instrumented prototypes, A/B tests, and post-launch telemetry—feed a learning flywheel that improves discovery priors and evaluation models over time. To ensure reliability, teams layer grounding data, verification/validation, and governance (e.g., criteria at gates, audit trails, bias checks), so AI augments creativity without sacrificing safety, ethics, or rigor. The result is more, better, and faster innovation with traceable reasoning and measurable impact.

- Discovery—mine signals of unmet need (e.g., unsupervised learning over search logs to reveal gaps in telemedicine)
- Generation—create rich option sets rapidly (e.g., large language models (LLMs), diffusion-based image models, topology optimization)
- Evaluation—use predictive models to rank opportunities and design concepts against preference, performance, or cost data, shortening loops

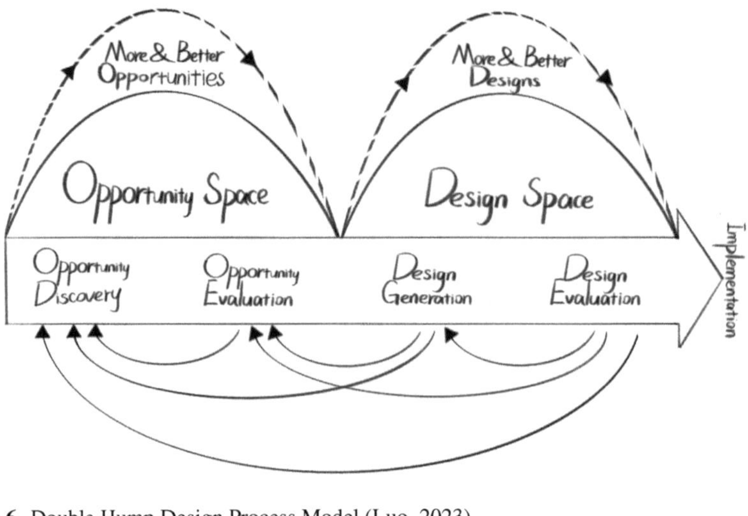

Fig. 3.6 Double Hump Design Process Model (Luo, 2023)

A Spectrum of Structure

Design processes are not one-size-fits-all. They span a spectrum—from tightly scripted, stage-gated systems to free-form, intuition-driven heuristics. At one end, systematic models such as Pahl and Beitz or Stage-Gate offer repeatability, traceability, and control, especially in regulated domains. At the other, adaptive and heuristic processes—design thinking, Lean Startup, or the Double Hump—offer flexibility and responsiveness to ambiguity, particularly in emerging or fast-evolving problem spaces.

Most real-world projects do not follow a single model from start to finish. Experienced teams blend models to match shifting needs. A project might begin with design thinking to explore user needs and reframe the brief transition to a Lean MVP loop to test fast and learn early and then shift to a Pahl and Beitz flow for detailed embodiment once investment stakes increase. A Stage-Gate system may be layered on to satisfy stakeholders or regulators, while AI-assisted methods—such as the Double Hump—are overlaid at key points to augment exploration and evaluation with data-driven insight. These hybrids embody a growing norm in practice: structured flexibility.

Over-reliance on rigid, linear processes can hinder innovation in high-uncertainty or creative contexts. Research in cognitive science—especially Gigerenzer's "adaptive toolbox"—shows that people often perform better when they can choose fast-and-frugal heuristics suited to context. In many cases, design teams using such heuristics have outperformed those constrained by overly prescriptive, general-purpose models (Magee & Frey, 2006). The implication is clear: design is not merely a process to follow, but a practice to interpret.

While academia and industry have trended toward more formalized models, many accomplished designers resist strict adherence. They argue that excellence stems less from a fixed diagram than from tacit judgment developed through experience. Some of the strongest critiques of teaching a single "universal" process come from master practitioners turned educators. Rather than enforcing one model, they advocate process literacy—the ability to understand multiple models, diagnose a project's demands, and assemble an appropriate hybrid.

The figure that follows (Fig. 3.7) maps common design models along two axes—uncertainty and cost of late change—as a heuristic for process selection. The best teams do not worship process diagrams; they wield them judiciously. They know when to explore, when to converge, and when to adapt—letting the process evolve alongside their understanding of the problem and the opportunity.

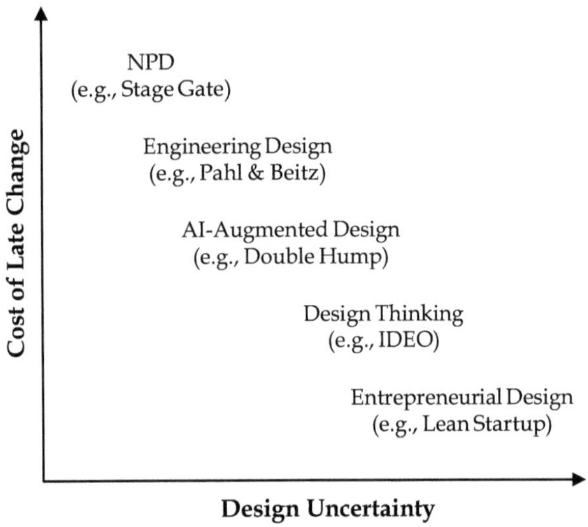

Fig. 3.7 Design Process models by uncertainty and cost of late change

Navigating the Landscape of Design Processes

No single design process is universally optimal. The right approach depends on the level of uncertainty, the timing of key decisions, and the stakes involved—especially when regulatory or technical constraints are high. More important than the label—"Design Thinking," "Build-Measure-Learn," or "Discover-Define-Develop-Deliver"—is the underlying rhythm of design: iterative alternation between divergence and convergence, between exploration and refinement. That fundamental structure underpins all effective processes.

Heuristics and human judgment remain indispensable, particularly in exploratory or high-novelty projects where rigid frameworks can stifle creativity. Fast, frugal experimentation often outperforms procedural complexity. As artificial intelligence increasingly augments design, it does not replace discernment, adaptability, or context-sensitive thinking; rather, it raises the bar on how we gather evidence, shorten feedback loops, and govern decisions.

In the end, design process is a means, not an end—a vehicle for transforming knowledge into value. Whatever path a team takes, the shared aim is the same: to turn discovery into usable invention and invention into widespread impact. The chapters that follow build on this logic, detailing principles and tools that help teams choose—and adapt—their process with intent.

References

Boehm, B. W. (1988). A spiral model of software development and enhancement. *ACM SIGSOFT Software Engineering Notes, 11*(4), 14–24.
Brown, T. (2008). Design thinking. *Harvard Business Review, 86*(6), 84–92.

Cooper, R. G. (1990). Stage-Gate systems: A new tool for managing new products. *Business Horizons, 33*(3), 44–54.

Forsberg, K., Mooz, H., & Cotterman, H. (2005). *Visualizing project management: Models and frameworks for mastering complex systems* (3rd ed.). Wiley.

Luo, J. (2023). Data-driven innovation: What is it? *IEEE Transactions on Engineering Management, 70*(2), 784–790.

Magee, C. L., & Frey, D. (2006). Experimentation and its role in engineering design. *International Journal of Engineering Education, 21*(3), 1–11.

Pahl, G., & Beitz, W. (2007). *Engineering design: A systematic approach.* Springer.

Ries, E. (2011). *The lean startup: How today's entrepreneurs use continuous innovation to create radically successful businesses.* Crown Business.

Stanford d.school. (2022). *An introduction to design thinking: Process guide.* Hasso Plattner Institute of Design at Stanford University.

Ulrich, K., & Eppinger, S. (2011). *Product design and development* (5th ed.). McGraw-Hill.

Chapter 4
Design Ontology

Abstract Ontologies make design reasoning explicit and computable. We survey four pillars—Function-Behavior-Structure (FBS), Axiomatic Design, Concept-Knowledge (C-K) Theory, and Theory of Inventive Problem Solving (TRIZ)—plus complementary formalisms. The chapter shows how functions, behaviors, structures, concepts, contradictions, and mappings encode design moves, support simulation and automation, and scaffold human–AI collaboration. Readers learn when and how to apply each ontology, and how ontological clarity improves traceability, creativity, and cross-team interoperability.

What Is Design Ontology

Design ontology is the formal specification of the concepts and relationships that define the nature of design—what entities exist, how they interact, and how they evolve through a process. It provides philosophical and methodological footing for structuring design theories, processes, and tools. As ontology in philosophy concerns the nature of being and existence, design ontology articulates the fundamental elements and logic that constitute the design space.

Design ontology underpins how we model and represent design knowledge and reasoning. By identifying and formalizing key constructs—such as functions, behaviors, structures, and concepts—ontologies clarify how designers think, decide, and create artifacts. They establish a shared vocabulary for design research and practice, support computational models of designing, and enable systematic, teachable design methods.

This chapter surveys several influential design ontologies, each offering a distinctive lens and operational abstraction:

- Function-Behavior-Structure (FBS)
- Axiomatic Design
- Concept-Knowledge (C-K) Design Theory
- Theory of Inventive Problem Solving (TRIZ)

J. Luo, *Design Science*, Applied Innovation and Technology Management,
https://doi.org/10.1007/978-3-032-13353-3_4

Beyond these four, we briefly consider additional ontologies and formalisms—including Design Science Research (DSR), General Design Theory (GDT), Object-Process Methodology (OPM), Activity Theory, and the ontological assumptions underlying design thinking—to situate the landscape and illustrate how these perspectives complement one another.

Together, these frameworks help us reason explicitly about design moves and transformations, align methods to problem structure, and connect human creativity with computable representations, which are foundations for rigorous analysis and effective innovation.

Function-Behavior-Structure (FBS)

The Function-Behavior-Structure (FBS) ontology, developed by John Gero (1990), provides a foundational framework for modeling and understanding the design process, particularly in engineering and architecture contexts. It formalizes three core constructs that represent the key elements of design reasoning:

- Function (F): What the artifact is intended to do—the purposes or goals it is meant to achieve. Function is tied to user needs and problem statements, often expressed in abstract terms (e.g., "support weight," "transmit force," or "enable motion").
- Behavior (B): How the artifact fulfills its function—the causal mechanisms, operations, or actions it exhibits. Behavior may be described in terms of physics (e.g., stress distribution), performance (e.g., efficiency), or logical outcomes.
- Structure (S): The actual configuration or form of the artifact—the arrangement of materials, components, and geometry that give rise to its behavior.

The FBS framework views design as an iterative, dynamic transformation of intentions into realizations through interrelated reasoning activities. Mappings among three central constructs—Function (F), Behavior (B), and Structure (S)—drive the formulation, synthesis, analysis, evaluation, and reformulation of design ideas (illustrated in Fig. 4.1).

The process typically proceeds as follows:

- Formulation (F → Be): translate high-level functions—what the artifact is meant to achieve—into expected behaviors (Be), often stated as performance targets or physical principles (e.g., the function "reduce drag" maps to a drag coefficient threshold or flow regime).
- Synthesis (Be → S): generate candidate structures (S)—configurations of components, materials, and geometry—intended to produce the expected behaviors. This is where abstract goals begin to take tangible form.
- Analysis (S → Bs): predict derived behaviors (Bs)—what the artifact actually does—using modeling, simulation, or empirical testing.
- Evaluation (Be ↔ Bs): compare predicted/measured behavior with expectations; identify performance gaps and trade-offs.

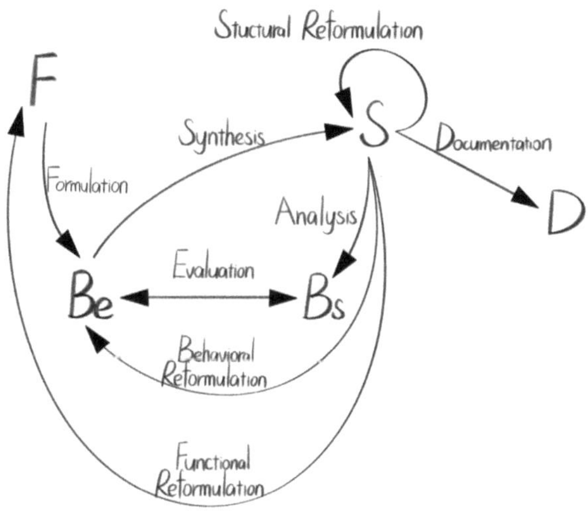

Fig. 4.1 The Function-Behavior-Structure Ontology (Gero, 1990)

Throughout this process, the FBS framework supports multiple forms of reformulation:

- Structure reformulation (S → S): modify the structure to better achieve the desired behavior.
- Behavior reformulation (S → Be): revise behavioral expectations in light of what the structure can realistically deliver.
- Function reformulation (S → F): rethink the original function based on new insights into the problem or solution space.

The final step, documentation (S → D), records the resulting structure and decisions in a form suitable for communication, fabrication, and verification, completing the design loop.

FBS captures the essence of design as an evolving, iterative, and often nonlinear process in which ideas and prototypes are continually tested, refined, and reframed. It supports both top-down (goal-driven) and bottom-up (emergent) reasoning, reflecting real-world design practice. By distinguishing between what a design is intended to do (function), how it does it (behavior), and what it is (structure), FBS provides a rigorous vocabulary and logical architecture for analyzing and improving designing.

It bridges the abstract and the concrete—the conceptual and the physical—serving both as a descriptive model of how design happens and a prescriptive guide for how it can be supported and improved. To aid practice, standardized function vocabularies and flow-based function modeling operationalize the F–B–S linkage—connecting abstract functions to expected behaviors and candidate structures (Stone & Wood, 2000). Finally, FBS makes design cognition explicit and computable: the elements F, Be/Bs, and S can be encoded and manipulated to support design automation, AI-assisted reasoning, and collaborative platforms.

Axiomatic Design

Axiomatic Design, developed by Nam Pyo Suh (2001), is a prescriptive framework for guiding the design process with formal principles. It rests on two foundational axioms aimed at improving the clarity, efficiency, and robustness of engineering designs:

- Independence Axiom: maintain the independence of functional requirements.
- Information Axiom: minimize the information content of the design.

At the core of Axiomatic Design is the mapping between functional requirements (FRs)—what the system must achieve—and design parameters (DPs)—the means by which these functions are realized. Under the Independence Axiom, a good design allows each functional requirement to be satisfied independently by a corresponding design parameter. This yields an uncoupled design where changes to one parameter do not spill over to others. By contrast, coupled designs (with interdependent FRs/DPs) create complex interactions that can degrade performance, raise failure risk, and complicate maintenance.

Despite the label "axiom," this is a strong normative claim rather than a universal law. In many real systems, intentional coupling outperforms uncoupled or decoupled designs—for example when tight integration reduces weight and parts, improves dynamic performance, enables compliant mechanisms, or lowers total cost. In such cases, coupling is not a defect but a design choice that trades simplified control for superior system-level outcomes.

To operationalize this principle, Axiomatic Design uses design matrices to represent the relationship between FRs and DPs (see Fig. 4.2). These algebraic representations enable early diagnosis of complexity and interdependencies: a diagonal matrix indicates an uncoupled design with clean one-to-one mappings; a triangular matrix indicates a decoupled design, where functional independence is preserved with a specific sequence; a fully populated matrix signals a coupled design, generally undesirable.

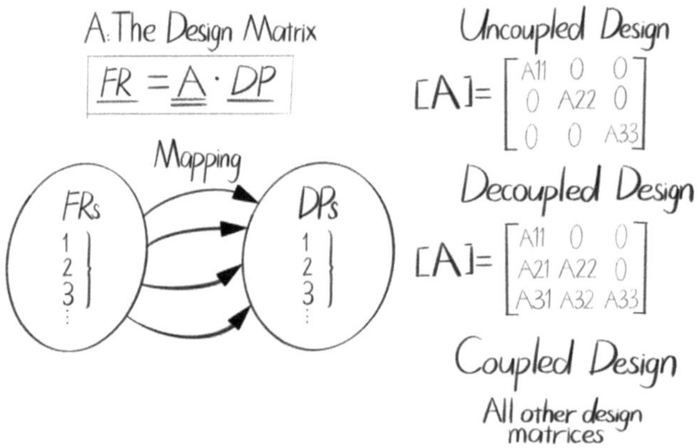

Fig. 4.2 Axiomatic Design: Design matrices and the function-to-design mapping (Suh, 2001)

The Information Axiom introduces a quantitative dimension to design evaluation. Among feasible alternatives, it advocates selecting the design with the lowest information content—equivalently, the highest probability of meeting all FRs within tolerance. Lower information content typically correlates with higher reliability, robustness, and manufacturability (e.g., designs with wider feasible ranges or less sensitivity to noise).

Minimizing information content presumes a stable environment and a single objective. In practice, higher formal complexity—through redundancy, reconfigurability, or rich control—can be the better alternative when robustness, safety, adaptability, or lifecycle value dominate. What appears "complex" by the axiom's metric may deliver superior performance under uncertainty.

Together, the axioms form a two-pronged framework: the first ensures conceptual clarity and controllability; the second guides optimization under uncertainty. Axiomatic Design is particularly powerful in early-stage conceptual design and systems engineering, where managing complexity and preserving decomposability are critical.

Beyond the FR-DP mapping, Axiomatic Design is embedded in a broader four-domain model that formalizes the full trajectory of the design process. This model consists of:

- Customer Domain—capture customer needs (CNs)
- Functional Domain—specify functional requirements (FRs)
- Physical Domain—identify design parameters (DPs)
- Process Domain—define process variables (PVs) for implementation

Design proceeds through mappings across these domains: Customer Needs → Functional Requirements → Design Parameters → Process Variables. This layered progression provides a structured methodology for translating user desires into manufacturable and testable artifacts. It bridges abstract intent and concrete realization.

Over time, this multi-domain framework has been generalized and applied across various disciplines—manufacturing systems, materials design, software architecture, organization design, and even business strategy. In each of these contexts, the axioms offer a unifying logic for structuring complexity, clarifying purpose, and minimizing unintended interactions among system elements.

Compared with ontologies like FBS, which model the cognitive and iterative nature of designing, Axiomatic Design is more normative and deterministic—offering clear criteria for assessing and improving design "goodness." It excels where functions and parameters can be explicitly defined and independently managed. In socio-technical systems or user-centered contexts—where requirements are interwoven and evolving—strict decoupling may need thoughtful adaptation.

Nam Suh's "axioms" should be read as powerful design heuristics, not inviolable truths. There exist well-documented counterexamples where (i) coupled designs are superior to uncoupled/decoupled alternatives, and (ii) greater complexity yields better robustness, adaptability, or performance. The practical stance is to apply the axioms as default preferences—then justify deviations when integration or complexity demonstrably improves system value.

Nonetheless, Axiomatic Design remains a foundational contribution to design science. It provides not only a theoretical basis for evaluating design quality but also a practical methodology for systematically progressing from needs to solutions across complex design domains.

Concept-Knowledge (C-K) Design Theory

Developed by Armand Hatchuel and Benoît Weil (2009), C-K Design Theory provides a high-level framework for modeling the creative process in design. Unlike design approaches that optimize within a predefined problem space, C-K formalizes how novelty emerges by structuring the unknown and enabling its exploration.

At the heart of the theory is a dual-space co-expansion consisting of two interdependent, evolving spaces (Fig. 4.3):

- C-space (Concepts): This space contains concepts—propositions that are neither true nor false yet. These are imaginative, undetermined design ideas that lack a known solution or logical status (e.g., a car that can fly, a spoon that never spills). Concepts are not vague wishes but structured starting points for creative reasoning.
- K-space (Knowledge): This space represents validated knowledge—facts, laws, principles, technologies, and prior solutions that are considered true within a given domain.

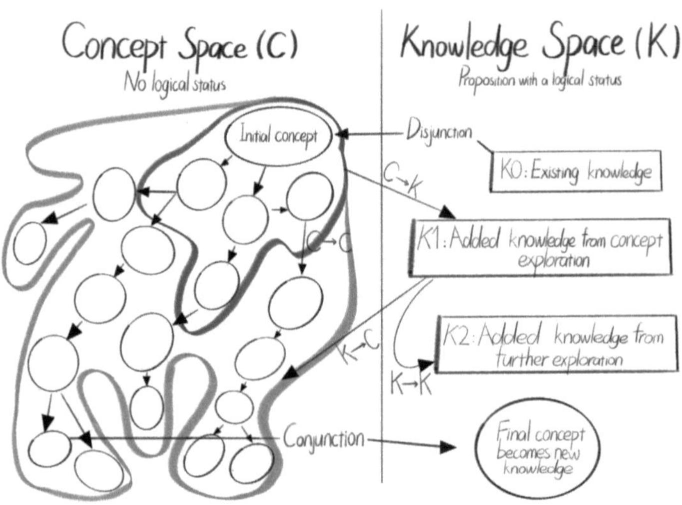

Fig. 4.3 Co-expansion of the concept-knowledge spaces (Hatchuel & Weil, 2009)

Creativity arises through a recursive dialogue between the concept and knowledge spaces.

- C → K: Concepts in the C-space stimulate exploration in the K-space. For example, the concept of a "flying car" activates the search for new relevant knowledge—such as lightweight materials, vertical takeoff technologies, or battery propulsion systems.
- K → C: Discoveries or recombinations in the K-space, in turn, lead to refinements, bifurcations, or expansions in the C-space. For instance, advancements in autonomous navigation or AI may give rise to new variants of the original concept—such as self-flying taxis or modular aerial vehicles.

This recursive dialogue between concept generation and knowledge activation makes C-K Theory particularly suited for radical innovation, where the objective is not just to find optimal solutions to known problems, but to reframe problems, challenge assumptions, and create new value spaces. C-K Theory does not assume the design space is fully defined at the outset; it evolves with the reasoning process.

A key contribution of C-K is showing how unknowns are progressively structured and resolved. It treats "not knowing" not as a gap or weakness but as a fertile condition for innovation. This ontological stance allows C-K to handle breakthrough thinking, cross-disciplinary ideation, and the redefinition of design problems in dynamic or ambiguous contexts.

C-K also provides a set of logical operators and partitioning rules that guide concept evolution—splitting concepts into sub-concepts, exploring alternatives, and steering searches. Typical moves include:

- Expansion: enlarging C and K spaces by introducing new attributes, analogies, or domains
- Conjunction: stabilizing a concept into knowledge (C → K) once validated
- Disjunction: reopening stabilized knowledge to generate fresh concepts (K → C)

These operators help designers manage complexity while maintaining creativity. In practice, C-K has been applied across diverse domains—from engineering and product design to public policy, organizational change, and strategic foresight. Its emphasis on conceptual exploration and knowledge mobilization suits interdisciplinary teams tackling open-ended or ill-structured problems.

C-K reframes design as a process of structured exploration of the unknown, bridging imagination and rigor. By making the interaction between concepts and knowledge explicit, it offers both a descriptive account of innovation dynamics and a prescriptive methodology for fostering creative breakthroughs.

Theory of Inventive Problem Solving (TRIZ)

TRIZ, an acronym derived from the Russian *Teoriya Resheniya Izobretatelskikh Zadach* (Theory of Inventive Problem Solving), was developed by Soviet inventor Genrich Altshuller (1984). Through a meticulous analysis of over 300,000 patents (of which roughly 40,000 represented genuine inventive breakthroughs), Altshuller and colleagues distilled repeatable patterns of innovation that cut across technologies and domains.

At its core, TRIZ challenges the idea that invention is domain-specific or random. Most breakthroughs, it argues, arise from solving design contradictions—situations where improving one attribute worsens another (e.g., increasing strength raises weight; improving precision slows throughput). Whereas traditional engineering often accepts such trade-offs, TRIZ provides systematic methods to resolve contradictions, aiming for higher performance without compromise.

This insight grounds TRIZ's ontological framework in empirical analysis rather than abstraction. Its key constructs—technical contradictions, inventive principles, and laws of technical system evolution—equip designers with a structured toolkit for innovation. By framing problems as recurring patterns with proven resolution strategies, TRIZ turns invention from a mysterious spark into a learnable, repeatable process.

Contradiction Matrix and Inventive Principles

TRIZ is operationalized most visibly through the contradiction matrix and the 40 inventive principles (Fig. 4.4). The matrix maps typical engineering parameters—such as weight, temperature, strength, speed, accuracy, and reliability—against one another to surface principles that have historically resolved similar conflicts. The classic matrix spans 39 parameters, yielding a 39 × 39 grid of 1482 potential contradictions.

Total 39 Technical Features

Improving Feature / Worsening Feature		Weight of moving object 1	Weight of stationary object 2	Length of moving object 3	Length of stationary object 4	Area of moving object 5	Area of stationary object 6	Volume of moving object 7	Volume of stationary object 8	Speed 9	Force (Intensity) 10	....	Extent of automation 38	Productivity 39
Weight of moving object	1	+		15, 8, 29,34		29, 17, 38, 34		29, 2, 40, 28		2, 8, 15, 38	8, 10, 18, 37	...	26, 35 18, 19	35, 3, 24, 37
Weight of stationary object	2		+		10, 1, 29, 35		35, 30, 13, 2		5, 35, 14, 2		8, 10, 19, 35	...	2, 26, 35	1, 28, 15, 35
Length of moving object	3	8, 15, 29, 34		+		15, 17, 4		7, 17, 4, 35		13, 4, 8	17, 10, 4	...	17, 24, 26, 16	14, 4, 28, 29
Length of stationary object	4		35, 28, 40, 29		+		17, 7, 10, 40		35, 8, 2,14		28, 10	...		30, 14, 7, 26
Area of moving object	5	2, 17, 29, 4		14, 15, 18, 4		+		7, 14, 17, 4		29, 30, 4, 34	19, 30, 35, 2	...	14, 30, 28, 23	10, 26, 34, 2
Area of stationary object	6		30, 2, 14, 18		26, 7, 9, 39		+				1, 18, 35, 36	...	23	10, 15, 17, 7
Volume of moving object	7	2, 26, 29, 40		1, 7, 4, 35		1, 7, 4, 17		+		29, 4, 38, 34	15, 35, 36, 37	...	35, 34, 16, 24	10, 6, 2, 34
Volume of stationary object	8		35, 10, 19, 14	19, 14	35, 8, 2, 14				+		2, 18, 37	...		35, 37, 10, 2
Speed	9	2, 28, 13, 38		13, 14, 8		29, 30, 34		7, 29, 34		+	13, 28, 15, 19	...	10, 18	
Force (Intensity)	10	8, 1, 37, 18	18, 13, 1, 28	17, 19, 9, 36	28, 10	19, 10, 15	1, 18, 36, 37	15, 9, 12, 37	2, 36, 18, 37	13, 28, 15, 12	+	...	2, 35	3, 28, 35, 37
......	...	...	...	...	...	...	...	...	...	...	...	...	...	...
Extent of automation	38	28, 26, 18, 35	28, 26, 35, 10	14, 13, 17, 28	23	17, 14, 13		35, 13, 16		28, 10	2, 35	...	+	5, 12, 35, 26
Productivity	39	35, 26, 24, 37	28, 27, 15, 3	18, 4, 28, 38	30, 7, 14, 26	10, 26, 34, 31	10, 35, 17, 7	2, 6, 34, 10	35, 37, 10, 2		28, 15, 10, 36	...	5, 12, 35, 26	+

Total 40 Solution Principles

1. Segmentation
2. Extraction, Separation, Removal, Segregation
3. Local Quality
4. Asymmetry
5. Combining, Integration, Merging
6. Universality, Multi-functionality
7. Nesting
8. Counterweight, Levitation
9. Preliminary anti-action, Prior counteraction
10. Prior action
11. Cushion in advance, compensate before

......

39. Inert environment or atmosphere
40. Composite materials

Fig. 4.4 Part of the contradiction matrix and inventive principles (Altshuller, 1984)

Each matrix cell points to one or more of the 40 inventive principles—heuristic strategies extracted from successful patents (e.g., segmentation, inversion, universality, dynamism). Together, the matrix and principles form a structured ideation tool: when facing a trade-off, designers consult the matrix to discover principles that have resolved analogous contradictions, systematically reusing cross-domain innovation knowledge.

Laws of Technical System Evolution

Beyond contradictions, TRIZ introduces laws of technical system evolution—generalized trends observed across technologies (Table 4.1). These laws describe predictable pathways of change and provide strategic foresight for proactive design.

At the core is the Law of Increasing Ideality, which asserts that systems tend to evolve toward delivering greater benefits while reducing cost and harm. Although perfect ideality is unattainable, successive design iterations move systems closer to

Table 4.1 Laws of technical system evolution in TRIZ

Law	Description	Design implication
Increasing Ideality	Systems evolve to maximize useful functions while minimizing costs and harms. Ideality = Benefits / (Costs + Harms)	Design should aim for higher functionality with lower resource consumption and fewer side effects
Uneven Development of Subsystems	Different parts of a system evolve at different rates, causing internal contradictions	Recognize and resolve subsystem mismatches to advance overall system performance
Transition to Super-System	When a system reaches limits of improvement, it becomes part of a larger super-system	Embed systems into broader contexts to unlock new capabilities and synergies
Increasing Dynamism and Controllability	Systems evolve from rigid to more dynamic and controllable structures	Introduce adjustable, responsive, or reconfigurable components to enhance adaptability
Matching of Rhythms	System components synchronize in timing, speed, or cycles for optimal function	Design for timing coordination among interacting parts to reduce inefficiencies
Transition from Macro to Micro-Level	Functions shift from macro- to micro- or nano-scale implementation	Explore finer physical scales and precision engineering for functional innovation
Increasing Use of Energy Fields	Systems evolve by utilizing more advanced energy fields (e.g., mechanical → electrical → electromagnetic → nuclear)	Investigate newer energy modalities for enhanced control, efficiency, or miniaturization
Shortening of Energy Flow Path	Energy and information transfer become more direct and efficient	Minimize intermediate elements or steps in function delivery to optimize performance

this goal. The Law of Uneven Development of Subsystems explains how components evolve at different rates, generating contradictions that drive further innovation. When a system reaches its limits, the Law of Transition to a Super-System suggests it becomes part of a larger system, opening new directions for evolution, such as the convergence of cameras and phones.

Several laws focus on structural and functional change. The Law of Increasing Dynamism and Controllability highlights a shift from rigid to more flexible and responsive designs, such as adaptive suspension systems. The Law of Matching Rhythms emphasizes synchronization between subsystems, ensuring cohesive performance. The Law of Transition from Macro to Micro-Level captures the trend toward miniaturization, enabling breakthroughs in precision technologies like semiconductor chips. The Law of Increasing Use of Energy Fields tracks the progression from mechanical to electromagnetic and nuclear energies, pointing to emerging modalities such as quantum or bioenergy. Lastly, the Law of Shortening of Energy Flow Path observes that systems evolve to minimize intermediaries in transferring energy or information, enhancing efficiency, as seen in direct-drive or integrated systems.

These laws are both descriptive (explaining how systems have evolved) and prescriptive (guiding next steps). Aligning designs with these trajectories helps generate innovations that are not only inventive but also in harmony with the natural trajectory of technological progress.

Automating TRIZ with AI

Despite its power, TRIZ has a steep learning curve. Mastery requires fluency with multiple constructs—contradiction matrices, inventive principles, and evolution laws—which can burden novices and slow adoption outside expert settings. To lower this barrier, researchers have begun automating TRIZ reasoning with AI.

One example is AutoTRIZ (Jiang et al., 2025), a framework that uses large language models (LLMs) to interpret natural-language problem statements, identifies underlying contradictions, maps them to TRIZ representations, selects relevant inventive principles, and generates candidate solutions. By embedding TRIZ heuristics in generative AI models, such tools make the method more accessible to non-experts and easier to integrate into modern, AI-assisted design workflows—illustrating how traditional design ontologies can be augmented at scale.

Additional Design Ontologies

Beyond the four foundational ontologies—FBS, Axiomatic Design, C-K Theory, and TRIZ—the broader field of design science includes other ontologically grounded frameworks that illuminate how design knowledge is structured, represented, and enacted. These perspectives arise from diverse traditions—information systems, engineering design, systems engineering, artificial intelligence, and human–computer interaction—reflecting the growing breadth and maturity of design theory.

One notable contribution is the Design Science Research (DSR) framework. With roots in Herbert Simon (1996) and formalized in information systems by Hevner et al. (2004), DSR articulates how knowledge is produced through the building and evaluation of purposeful artifacts. It emphasizes the interplay among theory, context, and design via three linked cycles: the relevance cycle (connecting to real-world application), the rigor cycle (anchoring in prior knowledge), and the design cycle (artifact creation and assessment). While not "ontological" in a strict philosophical sense, DSR provides a high-level structure for organizing design activities across research and practice, especially in digital innovation and business.

Another formal perspective is offered by General Design Theory (GDT). Proposed by Takeda et al. (1990), GDT formalizes relationships among function, structure, and requirements using abstract mathematical sets and mappings. It treats designing as transformations within a symbolic space, aligning naturally with computational design and AI-based reasoning. Although highly abstract, GDT is foundational for algorithmic approaches and formal logic models of design behavior.

In engineering design, the SAPPhIRE model of causality, introduced by Srinivasan, Chakrabarti, and Lindemann (2006), represents system behavior through seven constructs—State, Action, Part, Phenomenon, Input, oRgan, and Effect—linked in causal chains. It provides an ontology for capturing how inputs and phenomena combine with components to produce effects, supporting design-by-analogy, knowledge reuse, and computational reasoning. By emphasizing causality across technical and biological systems, SAPPhIRE enriches the ontological foundations of design science.

In systems engineering, Dov Dori (2002) introduced Object-Process Methodology (OPM)—a unified, visual-and-formal modeling language that integrates structure and behavior. Its core primitives are objects (what exists) and processes (how change occurs). OPM captures complex system interactions across levels of abstraction and has been standardized as ISO 19450, underscoring its relevance for industrial-scale systems design.

Activity Theory, originally developed in Soviet psychology and adapted by Yrjö Engeström (1987), provides a socio-technical lens on design in practice. It models systems in terms of subjects, tools, community, rules, and division of labor, highlighting the cultural and institutional embeddedness of designers and users. It is widely applied in human–computer interaction (HCI), participatory design, and organizational innovation. While not a design ontology narrowly defined, it offers an ontological framing of activity that is highly pertinent to real-world design contexts.

Design thinking frameworks, although often presented as process models, also carry implicit ontological assumptions. Centered on empathy, iteration, and user-centered problem framing, they assume a world where human needs, experiential understanding, and prototype-driven learning define what "design" is. In service design and innovation education, they function as both cognitive tools and cultural paradigms. Recent work increasingly formalizes their constructs and representations.

These additional ontologies broaden our understanding of design as a socio-technical, cognitive, and systemic endeavor—not merely a technical one. Each contributes a distinctive lens for framing problems, generating and applying knowledge, and structuring creativity. As design increasingly intersects with digital transformation, artificial intelligence, and sustainability, this diversified ontological foundation will be critical for advancing design theory and practice in the twenty-first century.

The Evolving Role of Ontology in Design

Design ontologies are the scaffolds that organize and formalize the knowledge, reasoning, and structure underlying design. By defining essential entities—functions, behaviors, structures, parameters, concepts, contradictions—and the relationships among them, they provide a rigorous frame for analyzing how design happens and how it can be improved. An ontological lens enables the abstraction, communication, and computation of design knowledge, making it possible to teach design more systematically, compare methodologies more meaningfully, and build tools that support or automate creative problem-solving.

As artificial intelligence becomes more deeply integrated into design practice, ontologies will play an even more pivotal role. They bridge human and machine reasoning by giving AI systems shared representations with which to encode, interpret, and participate in complex design activities. Ontologies can shape design knowledge bases, guide the orchestration of AI agents, and enable explainable, adaptive automation. Looking ahead, the evolution of design ontologies, in both theory and implementation, will be critical to how designers and machines co-create in increasingly complex, dynamic, and multidisciplinary environments.

References

Altshuller, G. S. (1984). *Creativity as an exact science: The theory of the solution of inventive problems*. Gordon and Breach.

Dori, D. (2002). *Object-process methodology – A holistic systems paradigm*. Springer.

Engeström, Y. (1987). *Learning by expanding: An activity-theoretical approach to developmental research*. Orienta-Konsultit.

Gero, J. S. (1990). Design prototypes: A knowledge representation schema for design. *AI Magazine, 11*(4), 26–36.

Hatchuel, A., & Weil, B. (2009). C-K design theory: An advanced formulation. *Research in Engineering Design, 19*(4), 181–192.

Hevner, A. R., March, S. T., Park, J., & Ram, S. (2004). Design science in information systems research. *MIS Quarterly, 28*(1), 75–105.

Jiang, S., Li, W., Qian, Y., Zhang, Y., & Luo, J. (2025). AutoTRIZ: Automating engineering innovation with TRIZ and large language models. *Advanced Engineering Informatics, 65*, 103312.

Simon, H. A. (1996). *The sciences of the artificial* (3rd ed.). MIT Press.

Srinivasan, V., Chakrabarti, A., & Lindemann, U. (2006). Towards an ontology of engineering design using SAPPhIRE model. *Research in Engineering Design, 17*(4), 185–199.

Suh, N. P. (2001). *Axiomatic design: Advances and applications*. Oxford University Press.

Takeda, H., Yoshioka, M., Tomiyama, T., & Yoshikawa, H. (1990). Modeling design processes. *AI Magazine, 11*(4), 37–48.

Chapter 5
Design Creativity

Abstract Creativity in design is the capacity to generate and realize ideas that are both novel and appropriate to purpose, context, and constraints. This chapter reviews levels of creativity, core cognitive mechanisms (abduction, analogy, recombination), and enabling conditions across individuals, teams, and organizations. We connect creative practice to evidence-seeking (prototyping) and decision-making (convergence), highlight the role of craftsmanship in making ideas real, and show how AI can widen search and accelerate iteration while human judgment guards meaning, values, and trade-offs.

What Is Creativity in Design

Creativity lies at the heart of design—the ability to generate and realize ideas that are both novel and useful. In design, creativity is contextual: ideas must be original and aligned with user needs, technical constraints, and implementation pathways. Unlike artistic creativity, which may celebrate radical novelty or personal expression, design creativity is purpose-driven. It aims to improve lives, systems, products, and experiences in ways that are meaningful, feasible, and sustainable.

Design creativity often operates under ill-structured conditions, where neither the problem nor the solution is clearly defined. It is fueled by abductive reasoning—the capacity to imagine what could be even when precedent is thin. Yet, in practice, progress comes from retrieving relevant experience, reframing representations, and adapting prior solutions to fit emerging constraints. It requires ordinary cognitive process of memory, attention, and adaptation rather than mysterious leaps (Weisberg, 2006). Consequently, creativity is central not only to early ideation but also to problem-framing, iteration, prototyping, and decision-making throughout the design process.

J. Luo, *Design Science*, Applied Innovation and Technology Management,
https://doi.org/10.1007/978-3-032-13353-3_5

Types of Creativity

Creativity is not monolithic. It spans different scales, influences, and contexts. A widely cited model by Kaufman and Beghetto (2009) distinguishes four types—mini-c, little-c, Pro-c, and Big-C—based on scope and perceived impact.

Mini-c creativity describes the personal "aha" moments that arise in learning and sense-making. The novelty here is subjective: it may be familiar to the field, yet it is newly discovered by the individual and therefore meaningful. Think of a design student who, while experimenting in studio, stumbles upon an unexpected material configuration that behaves just right. These sparks build confidence, deepen tacit understanding, and often seed the habits of inquiry that mature into expertise.

Little-c creativity lives in the fabric of everyday problem-solving. It shows up in small but consequential improvements that enhance daily life, such as rearranging a workspace to minimize reach and motion, or devising a quick workaround to stabilize a shaky prototype before user testing. Modest in scope, little-c is essential for user-centered adaptation: it tunes systems to real contexts and keeps teams moving despite constraints.

Pro-c creativity emerges when domain expertise and professional recognition. Here, creators work from a deep well of knowledge and craft, producing contributions that peers acknowledge as advancements, such as an original mechanism that improves performance, an interface that wins awards for accessibility, or a construction method that measurably reduces embodied carbon. Reaching pro-c typically takes years of deliberate practice, critique, and iteration; mastery becomes a platform for systematic, reliable invention.

Big-c creativity denotes the rare breakthroughs that reconfigure disciplines or reshape society. These are the field-defining moves, such as Leonardo da Vinci's speculative machines, the iPhone's integration of multi-touch computing and a developer ecosystem, or Elon Musk's reimagining of space travel. Big-c outcomes often reflect systemic thinking and are recognized over time, as their ripple effects accumulate across technologies, markets, and everyday life.

Designers can operate across these levels over time or even within a single project. A student's material exploration shows mini-c; a user's clever workaround illustrates little-c; a patentable feature contributes Pro-c; and a team that redefines a product category demonstrates Big-C. Understanding these types helps educators, practitioners, and organizations tailor support: nurture learning (mini-c), celebrate everyday ingenuity (little-c), cultivate expertise (Pro-c), and invest in transformative potential (Big-C).

Sources of Creativity

Creativity in design emerges from a rich interplay of internal insight and external stimulus. By understanding its diverse sources, designers can better cultivate environments that foster it. Six common sources frequently underpin creative practice: personal experience, analogical thinking, constraints, collaboration, serendipity, and intrinsic motivation.

Personal experience often sits at the root of original ideas, arising from firsthand encounters with unmet needs or everyday frustrations—what Don Norman calls "design opportunities in the wild." Lived experience sharpens intuition and fosters empathy, turning vague discomfort into concrete problem statements and actionable constraints. The Embrace infant warmer is a well-known illustration: after witnessing the realities of off-grid hospitals, where conventional incubators were unavailable or impractical, the team reframed the challenge and pursued a radically simpler, context-appropriate solution.

Analogy is a powerful engine of creativity: by importing insights from distant domains, designers reframe constraints and surface fresh options. Biomimicry is emblematic—Velcro from burrs that cling to fur, and the Shinkansen's quieter nose from a kingfisher's beak. The leap is structured, with mapping functions rather than copying forms to yield workable designs. Crucially, analogical transfer typically relies on retrieval cues, contextual fit, and careful adaptation rather than any special "genius" mechanism (Weisberg, 2006).

Constraints, paradoxically, are another powerful catalyst. Limitations of budget, time, materials, or regulation can push teams off default paths and toward inventive alternatives. Frugal innovation demonstrates how scarcity can become a design brief: when resources are tight, solutions are forced to be essential, modular, repairable, and contextually appropriate. The "box" of constraints does not merely hem in imagination; it provides edges against which imagination can gain traction.

Collaboration extends the search space by combining different ways of seeing and thinking. Diverse design teams—spanning backgrounds, disciplines, and lived experiences—are more likely to challenge assumptions, surface hidden requirements, and assemble partial insights into workable wholes. Creative performance here is not the sum of individual talents but the product of varied mental models interacting, often productively, in tension.

Serendipity plays a quieter but no less important role. Breakthroughs often appear during relaxed, open-ended exploration—sketching without judgment, tinkering with materials, or drifting through a conversation where curiosity rather than certainty leads. These moments depend on an uncluttered mind and an environment that welcomes ambiguity, curiosity, and play. Structure sets the stage; looseness lets insight walk on.

Finally, intrinsic motivation sustains the long, uneven arc from promising idea to delivered impact. When designers care deeply about a problem, they tolerate ambiguity, absorb setbacks, and take principled risks. Passion does not guarantee novelty, but it fuels the perseverance required for bold ideas to survive critique, iteration, and the grind of implementation. In practice, intrinsic motivation is the engine that keeps the creative process moving when external rewards are uncertain or delayed.

In sum, creativity is not a single process but a convergence of personal, social, and environmental factors (Hennessey & Amabile, 2010). By tapping these sources, designers stay open to inspiration from every corner of their context. These sources interact with the Four P's and the componential levers discussed next—a reminder that personal, process, and contextual factors work together.

Dimensions of Creativity

Creativity is shaped by multiple, interrelated factors. A durable framework for understanding them is Rhodes' (1961) Four P's: Person, Process, Press, and Product. The model highlights that creativity is not only about innate talent; it also depends on thinking patterns, context, and outcomes.

- Person—Personal traits and dispositions that support creative potential, such as openness to experience, curiosity, intrinsic motivation, and risk tolerance. While some people naturally show these qualities, many can be cultivated, e.g., repeated engagement with ambiguous or complex problems increases comfort with uncertainty.
- Process—The cognitive and behavioral mechanisms of creative work (e.g., preparation, incubation, insight, evaluation). In design, the process is rarely linear; it involves iterative cycles of ideation, prototyping, and reflection. Recognizing these dynamics helps teams structure workflows that sustain creativity.
- Press— Environmental influences, including physical space, social climate, and cultural attitudes toward risk and failure. Supportive environments—psychological safety, collaboration, and freedom to experiment—foster creativity, whereas rigid or judgmental settings suppress it.
- Product—The outcomes of creative activity: ideas, artifacts, and solutions. To be truly creative, a product must be both novel and valuable in context. In design, this ranges from intuitive interfaces to transformative technologies; evaluation therefore balances originality with utility and impact.

Taken together, the Four P's offer a holistic view of creativity. A talented individual (Person) may struggle in an unsupportive Press, just as a novel Product requires iterative Process to succeed. Addressing all four dimensions helps designers and educators cultivate creative capacity more effectively.

Components of Creativity

Building on the Four P's, the Componential Theory (Hennessey & Amabile, 2010) highlights three levers teams can develop—domain-relevant skills, creativity-relevant skills, and task motivation—that jointly shape creative performance in individuals and teams.

Domain-relevant skills refer to factual knowledge, technical expertise, and procedural know-how within a field. In design, this includes familiarity with materials, user needs, manufacturing processes, and aesthetic principles. Such foundations enable ideas that are both novel and viable. However, deep expertise can induce fixation; cross-domain exposure can counter this by fostering analogy and idea recombination.

Creativity-relevant skills encompass the cognitive and dispositional capacities that support originality—divergent thinking, mental flexibility, openness to experience, reframing ability, tolerance for ambiguity, and a willingness to experiment or take risks. While partly dispositional, these can be cultivated through reflective practice and varied design experiences.

Task motivation, especially intrinsic motivation—curiosity, enjoyment, personal meaning—is a powerful driver of creativity. Intrinsic motives promote deeper exploration, bolder risks, and persistence. By contrast, poorly structured extrinsic pressures (e.g., controlling evaluation, rigid deadlines) can suppress creativity by reducing autonomy or increasing anxiety.

Creativity does not reside solely within individuals; it emerges from the interplay between people and their environments. As Hennessey and Amabile (2010) note, neurological factors such as affect and cognition, personal traits like confidence and perseverance, and environmental conditions—including support for risk-taking—operate together. In practice, a supportive environment is foundational: organizational culture, leadership, and team climate that cultivate psychological safety, trust, and openness to experimentation make it easier to voice unconventional ideas.

To cultivate creativity, the following strategies may guide action:

- Nurture intrinsic motivation with meaningful, autonomous, engaging tasks.
- Build creativity-relevant skills through reflective practice, reframing techniques, and deliberate exposure to ambiguity.
- Develop deep and broad domain knowledge while avoiding overreliance on habitual patterns.
- Foster team cultures that embrace experimentation, tolerate failure, and reward curiosity.

Creativity thrives not in isolation but in ecosystems—where motivated individuals interact with enabling environments, tools, and collaborators. Intentionally shaping these components is essential to sustaining creativity in design. Practical ways to build these levers appear in the strategies section ("Fostering Creativity in Design") below.

Personalities of Creative Outliers

Studies of history's prolific inventors—Leonardo da Vinci, Thomas Edison, Nikola Tesla, Alexander Graham Bell, Albert Einstein, Steve Jobs, Elon Musk—reveal common threads in personality, thinking style, and problem-solving approach (Root-Bernstein & Root-Bernstein, 1999; Simonton, 1999). These figures were not narrow specialists; they combined deep technical fluency with broad intellectual curiosity and a habit of challenging convention.

A defining feature is a generalist orientation. They mastered core tools and methods yet refused to stay within disciplinary boundaries. Intrinsically motivated by problems rather than specific solutions, they treated knowledge as interconnected. Their breakthroughs often came not from polishing existing answers but from questioning assumptions, reframing problems, and seeking systemic rather than local solutions. In *Quirky* (2018), Melissa Schilling profiles eight breakthrough innovators (e.g., Einstein, Franklin, Edison, Jobs, Musk) and identifies recurring traits that fuel their creativity:

- High openness and intellectual curiosity: They relentlessly explored new domains and perspectives.
- Low agreeableness (constructive dissent): Their independence and willingness to defy consensus helped them resist conformity and groupthink.
- Strong self-efficacy and resilience: They believed deeply in their capacity to succeed, enabling them to persist through failure and skepticism.
- Idealism and sense of purpose: Many were motivated by a grand vision—whether scientific truth, human progress, or technological revolution—rather than personal gain alone.
- Selective social detachment: Their tendency to remain emotionally independent from peer approval gave them the psychological freedom to pursue unconventional paths.

Not every designer needs these traits in extreme form. But cultivating intellectual independence, intrinsic motivation, comfort with ambiguity, and resilience in the face of failure can meaningfully elevate creative potential. The lesson from outliers is not that geniuses are inborn, but that certain attitudes and behaviors—when consciously nurtured and supported—consistently foster innovation.

Actionable Process Model of Creativity

Creativity in design is neither conjuring ideas from nothing nor merely possessing vast information. A library holds immense knowledge but generates no ideas; a newborn has potential but lacks content to transform. In truth, creativity arises by transforming prior knowledge into something novel and useful. This points to a process-based model of creative ideation (Fig. 5.1).

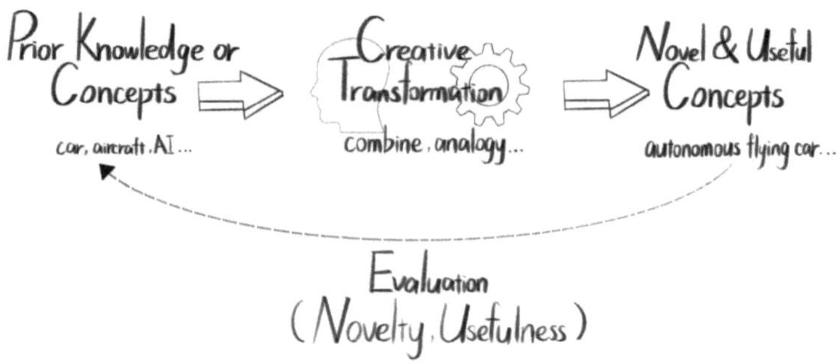

Fig. 5.1 Creative ideation: A process-based view

At its core, design creativity recombines, reconfigures, and transforms existing concepts, experiences, and insights into configurations that are both original and valuable. To transform knowledge creatively, one must first have a base of knowledge—whether experiential, disciplinary, and cross-domain. Creative heuristics act as catalysts, stimulating reinterpretation, activating analogies, and encouraging exploration beyond familiar boundaries.

The quality and diversity of one's knowledge base strongly shape creative potential. Designers need enough domain expertise to grasp problems and constraints—but not so much that they become locked into conventional thinking patterns. Cross-disciplinary knowledge is especially valuable for analogical reasoning and transfer across contexts (as in biomimicry, design by analogy, or lateral thinking).

Once ideas are generated, the next challenge is evaluation. What makes an idea truly creative? Most definitions agree: it must be novel and useful. Both criteria are context-dependent. Novelty is relative—what's new in one setting may be familiar in another. Ideas that cross disciplinary, temporal, or cultural boundaries can appear more novel because the recombination is unfamiliar. Usefulness depends on the needs and values of specific users. What helps an older adult may not matter to a teenager, and a solution that works in Japan may not resonate in the U.S.

This contextual variability underscores the central role of empathy in design creativity. To evaluate and refine ideas effectively, designers must understand the people and situations they are designing for. Empathy allows designers to anticipate needs, appreciate diverse values, and tailor solutions accordingly.

A vivid illustration is the selfie stick. In the 1990s, Japanese inventor Kenji Kawakami listed it among "Chindogu"—ingenious but useless inventions. Decades later, with smartphones and social media, the same idea became ubiquitous and useful. The concept did not change; context, timing, and user relevance did. Creative value shifts with empathy and environment.

To develop user empathy systematically, methods such as persona development, interviews, immersion, and other approaches can be employed. Empathy should extend beyond end users: design outcomes affect stakeholders—investors, collaborators, suppliers, regulators, media, even competitors. Understanding their incentives and constraints helps anticipate friction, align interests, and secure support for implementation.

In summary, and drawing on the earlier definition that human creativity is the ability to generate ideas that are novel and useful, three core components underpin a designer's creative capacity:

- A rich, diverse knowledge base enabling meaningful transformation
- Effective ideation heuristics that stimulate new ways of seeing and recombining
- Empathic insight into users and stakeholders to judge relevance and impact

This process model of creativity treats ideation not as a mystical flash but as a structured transformation of what we already know into outcomes that improve human experience. By deliberately cultivating knowledge, heuristics, and empathy, we can build the creative capacity needed for complex, evolving design challenges.

Cross-Domain Creativity and Knowledge Transformation

One of design's most powerful engines is the ability to cross disciplinary boundaries. Creativity is not mere application of knowledge but its transformation. In this light, cross-domain creativity—connecting ideas from disparate fields—becomes a key driver of breakthrough innovation. It rests on two essentials:

- Breadth of exposure: accumulating knowledge from diverse domains, systems, and metaphors.
- Cognitive flexibility: restructuring, reinterpreting, and recombining that knowledge in novel ways.

Analogical reasoning plays a central role. Effective analogy relies on structural alignment—mapping relational structure rather than surface features—so cross-domain transfers work when deep relations match, not merely appearances (Markman & Gentner, 1993). Designers regularly draw from nature, culture, and unrelated technologies to make creative leaps. Biomimicry yields Velcro from burrs, drones modeled on avian and insect flight, and passive building cooling inspired by termite mounds. These are not imitations but creative recombination enabled by mental agility and skillful use of analogy.

This perspective aligns with Amabile's Componential Theory, which argues that domain knowledge need not be siloed; transformative ideas often arise when concepts from one field are adapted to another. Likewise, Schilling's book *Quirky* (2018) profiles show how polymaths such as Elon Musk, Nikola Tesla, Thomas Edison, and Steve Jobs operated at intersections, drawing on overlapping interests to fuel cross-domain creativity.

To support this mode of creativity, design heuristics function as flexible cognitive bridges. Heuristics such as combine, substitute, reframe, and reverse prompt exploration of unexpected relationships and open new paths between existing ideas. Used reflectively, they amplify ideation under uncertainty and incomplete information.

Infused design theory (Shai & Reich, 2004) extends this logic by offering a formal framework for cross-domain creativity. Through abstract mathematical representations, it enables solutions from one discipline to be infused into another, breaking down silos and supporting concurrent engineering. By making knowledge transferable at a structural level rather than only through analogy, infused design complements heuristic exploration and strengthens the transformation of ideas across fields.

Technology can further operationalize cross-domain thinking. One example is InnoGPS (Luo et al., 2021), a computational tool for analogy and cross-domain inference. Inspired by the Google Maps paradigm, InnoGPS visualizes a technology space map of global knowledge domains. As normal maps let users locate themselves geographically and explore routes, InnoGPS lets designers, inventors, and organizations locate themselves in knowledge space and explore nearby or distant technological "neighborhoods."

The tool's core innovation is an empirically constructed map that organizes millions of patents by quantified knowledge distance—derived from citation links, co-classifications, and shared knowledge bases. This infrastructure provides a scaffold for creativity by analogy, guiding users toward proximate areas for incremental advances or distant regions for radical recombination. An automotive engineer, for instance, might explore aerospace or advanced materials for novel chassis architectures; a healthcare innovator might draw on digital entertainment to redesign patient engagement systems.

InnoGPS is itself a product of analogical design: its interface adapts Google Maps' logic to technological exploration. In place of streets and cities, InnoGPS maps technologies, inventors, and organizations. Instead of physical routes, it suggests paths of knowledge recombination. It is a design space navigation system for inventive exploration (Luo et al., 2017). AI tools extend this analogical search, as the next section shows.

Ultimately, tools like InnoGPS extend the natural powers of the creative mind. By externalizing knowledge distance, suggesting analogical directions, and supporting rapid idea generation, they operationalize the cognitive processes that drive human creativity. The result is a glimpse of augmented creativity: synergy between human intuition, heuristic reasoning, and intelligent infrastructure that makes the global innovation landscape more navigable, and more generative.

AI as a Creativity Amplifier

Traditionally, creative design has relied on human intuition, lived experience, and analogical thinking to transform prior knowledge into novel ideas. The rise of artificial intelligence (AI)—especially generative models such as large language models (LLMs)—is reshaping this landscape. These tools are not creative in the human sense, but they amplify creativity by expanding access to knowledge, accelerating ideation, and supporting transformation at scale.

AI's generative potential stems from training on massive, cross-domain data. Foundation models (FMs) encode rich domain knowledge and broad commonsense patterns, making them potent "knowledge-ready" assistants. With effective prompting or fine-tuning, LLMs can simulate analogical reasoning, surface design patterns, and generate conceptual variations. In effect, they act as externalized associative engines, recombining prior knowledge much as designers do via heuristics (Lou, 2023).

This makes AI a powerful catalyst for creative ideation—especially for those without decades of accumulated expertise. Humans must learn, synthesize, and store knowledge over time. AI can retrieve and recombine it instantly. This does not replace human creativity; it augments it, lowering the threshold for exploration and reducing the cost of trial and error.

In our recent research, we combined LLMs with InnoGPS to explore guided artificial creativity. By fine-tuning a generic LLM on patent datasets from diverse domains (e.g., agriculture, lighting, weapons), we created domain-specialist agents and tasked them with designing a rolling robot. The originality of outputs correlated with knowledge distance: agents trained on more distant domains generated more novel ideas (Zhu & Luo, 2022). In a related study, we emphasized reasoning strategy over knowledge scope: using a small, curated dataset of biologically inspired designs, we trained an LLM to simulate biomimetic reasoning—translating natural phenomena into engineered solutions (Zhu, et al., 2022). Despite limited data, the model internalized analogical patterns, showing that creative heuristics can be embedded in AI systems to guide concept generation.

Artificial Creativity: A Human-Centered Framework

If human creativity transforms prior knowledge through heuristics and empathy into novel, useful concepts (Fig. 5.1), artificial creativity can be framed similarly. Its effectiveness depends on three pillars:

- Knowledge base—the scale and diversity of training data
- Reasoning capability—the ability to manipulate, reframe, and analogize knowledge (heuristic-like thinking)
- Empathy and evaluation—the capacity to infer human needs and contexts and to assess novelty and usefulness

This framework points to AI-assisted ideation that is controllable and purposeful—guided by how we curate training data, structure reasoning, and define evaluative criteria. Yet, creativity is more than idea generation: it entails judgment, motivation, and value alignment. AI can propose thousands of options, but it cannot determine desirability, contextual fit, or ethical implications without human oversight.

The Role of Human Designers in an AI-Augmented Future

As AI becomes more capable, the human designer's role becomes more critical. Designers must curate data, craft prompts, interpret outputs, and—most importantly—set goals. AI is a powerful tool, not an autonomous creator; it lacks (and should not be given) intrinsic motivation, situated understanding, and value-based judgment. Designers remain leaders of the process, using AI as a co-creative partner.

Looking ahead, we must ensure that humans design the AI that supports human-centered design (Song et al., 2024). Design practitioners should wield AI safely, ethically, and intentionally—to inspire more original concepts, uncover promising opportunities, and deliver innovations that are not only novel but meaningful. In this emerging paradigm, creativity becomes a distributed, orchestrated process, where human and artificial intelligences converge to imagine—and realize—the future.

Fostering Creativity in Design

Creativity in design is not a mystical gift but a learnable, cultivable capacity. As this chapter shows, it emerges from the interplay of intrinsic motivation, domain knowledge, cognitive flexibility, heuristics, and enabling environments. It is both individual and systemic—shaped by inner drivers (curiosity, persistence) and outer conditions (education, culture, tools).

Educators and practitioners play a central role. The aim is not to impose rigid steps but to design environments, mindsets, and supports that encourage exploration, risk-taking, and meaningful experimentation. As Hennessey and Amabile (2010) emphasize, fostering creativity involves cultivating domain-relevant knowledge, creativity-relevant skills, and especially intrinsic motivation. Schilling (2018) further shows that outliers thrive on intense curiosity, unconventional thinking, and persistent engagement—traits that can be nurtured by well-designed learning and work contexts. To translate these insights into practice, design education and professional practice can adopt a range of proven strategies (Table 5.1):

Ultimately, fostering creativity in design means designing for creativity itself—thoughtfully structuring environments, processes, tools, and cultures. When these conditions are in place, novices and experts alike are more likely to produce ideas that are not only novel and feasible, but also meaningful and impactful.

Table 5.1 Actionable strategies to foster creativity

Strategies to foster creativity	Actionable guidelines
Teach design heuristics	Provide cognitive scaffolds (e.g., combine, substitute, reverse, analogize) to guide generative thinking
Promote cross-domain exposure	Encourage exploration across fields to expand analogies, metaphors, and conceptual tools
Support intrinsic motivation	Build cultures of autonomy, curiosity, and purpose to sustain engagement
Use divergent ideation tools	Apply SCAMPER, random-word prompts, morphological analysis, biomimicry, and similar methods to trigger unexpected associations
Leverage experiential methods	Use bodystorming, role-play, and sketching to surface insights and accelerate iteration
Normalize low-stakes experimentation	Make failure safe to enable playful exploration without fear of judgment
Reframe constraints	Treat limits as design prompts; designing under extremes can spark originality
Cultivate team creativity and dialogue	Ensure psychological safety, perspective diversity, shared goals, and reflective conversation
Integrate AI and digital tools	Use generative AI and InnoGPS to augment ideation, reveal hidden connections, and scale experimentation; these tools are amplifiers, not replacements

Creativity as the Engine of Design Innovation

Creativity is the driving force behind design innovation. It empowers designers to transcend the obvious, connect disparate ideas, and generate solutions that are both novel and meaningful. Far from an accidental spark, creativity emerges from the interplay of knowledge, motivation, reasoning, and context. Whether exercised by individuals or augmented by AI, it remains a purposeful act of transformation—turning what is known into what is possible. As design continues to meet uncertainty and complexity, creative capacity—human and AI-enabled—will determine our ability to innovate and shape a better future.

Creativity is not only ideation and empathy; it also demands craftsmanship—the skills, material fluency, and disciplined execution that turn possibilities into reliable realities. In the chapters ahead we first deepen the aims and the moves of creative work—empathy clarifies for whom and to what ends we create, and heuristics supplies the operating grammar under uncertainty. We then return to craft in prototyping, where thinking-through-making turns ideas into evidence, and in convergence, where disciplined choice and verification turn intent into commitments that hold in the world.

References

Hennessey, B. A., & Amabile, T. M. (2010). Creativity. *Annual Review of Psychology, 61*, 569–598.

Kaufman, J. C., & Beghetto, R. A. (2009). Beyond big and little: The four C model of creativity. *Review of General Psychology, 13*(1), 1–12.

Lou, Y. (2023). Human creativity in the AIGC era. *She Ji: The Journal of Design, Economics, and Innovation, 9*(4), 541–552.

Luo, J., Yan, B., & Wood, K. (2017). InnoGPS for data-driven exploration of design opportunities and directions: The case of Google driverless car project. *Journal of Mechanical Design, 139*(11), 111416.

Luo, J., Sarica, S., & Wood, K. (2021). Guiding data-driven design ideation by knowledge distance. *Knowledge-Based Systems, 218*, 106873.

Markman, A. B., & Gentner, D. (1993). Structural alignment during similarity comparisons. *Cognitive Psychology, 25*(4), 431–467.

Rhodes, M. (1961). An analysis of creativity. *The Phi Delta Kappan, 42*(7), 305–310.

Root-Bernstein, R., & Root-Bernstein, M. (1999). *Sparks of genius: The thirteen thinking tools of the world's most creative people*. Houghton Mifflin Harcourt.

Schilling, M. A. (2018). *Quirky: The remarkable story of the traits, foibles, and genius of breakthrough innovators who changed the world*. PublicAffairs.

Shai, O., & Reich, Y. (2004). Infused design. I. Theory. *Research in Engineering Design, 15*(2), 93–107.

Simonton, D. K. (1999). *Origins of genius: Darwinian perspectives on creativity*. Oxford University Press.

Song, B., Zhu, Q., & Luo, J. (2024). Human-AI collaboration by design. In *18th International Design Conference*, Dubrovnik, Croatia.

Weisberg, R. W. (2006). *Creativity: Understanding innovation in problem solving, science, invention, and the arts*. Hoboken, NJ: Wiley.

Zhu, Q., & Luo, J. (2022). Generative design ideation: A natural language generation approach. In *10th Conference on Design Computing and Cognition (DCC)*, Glasgow, UK.

Zhu, Q., Zhang, X., & Luo, J. (2022). Generative pre-trained transformer for biologically inspired design. In *ASME IDETC-CIE – 34th International Conference on Design Theory & Methodology,* St. Louis, Missouri, USA.

Chapter 6
Design Empathy

Abstract Empathy evolves from user-centered usability to human-centered dignity and humanity-centered sustainability. We treat empathy as skill, process, and moral stance—supported by rigorous methods and reflexive practice that avoids "empathy theater." The chapter frames limits and biases, then explores how AI can augment empathic reach at scale without replacing human care, emphasizing cultural sensitivity, accountability, and the embedding of equity and long-term stewardship in design criteria.

Why Empathy Matters in Design

Design is fundamentally a human endeavor. At its core, it seeks to improve lives by shaping artifacts, systems, and experiences that respond meaningfully to human needs, values, and aspirations. Among design competencies, empathy—the capacity to understand and engage with others' feelings, goals, and contexts—anchors the act of designing, giving it moral force and human relevance.

This chapter traces the evolution of empathy in design: from User-Centered Design (UCD) to Human-Centered Design (HCD) and, ultimately, to Humanity-Centered Design (HuCD). Drawing on frameworks such as the Kano Model, Quality Function Deployment (QFD), Kansei Engineering, core usability principles, and emerging practices in sustainable and ethical design, we examine empathy as both a practical methodology and an ethical compass. We also consider how a systems-aware empathy can guide more sustainable, inclusive, and responsible design.

From User-Centered Design to Empathy Development

User-Centered Design (UCD) emerged in the late twentieth century as a response to engineering-driven approaches that marginalized the lived experience of end users. UCD repositions the user as a primary source of design insight and evaluation. It

J. Luo, *Design Science*, Applied Innovation and Technology Management,
https://doi.org/10.1007/978-3-032-13353-3_6

emphasizes deep understanding of users' experiences, expectations, goals, frustrations, and cognitive and physical limits. Crucially, this is not just a philosophy but a methodology—using direct observation, contextual inquiry, persona development, journey mapping, and scenario testing to uncover not only what users do and say, but also what they feel and aspire to.

Empathy in UCD is cultivated through immersion in the user's world. Ethnographic shadowing can surface unspoken needs or latent pain points; journey mapping reveals friction and moments of delight across the experience; personas distill patterns into design-relevant archetypes. These practices help designers adopt the user's perspective and make decisions that are both emotionally resonant and intuitively usable. To systematize empathic insight, UCD employs several structured frameworks.

Kano Model, introduced by Noriaki Kano, distinguishes basic needs (whose absence causes dissatisfaction), performance needs (satisfaction scales with performance), and delighters (unexpected features that delight) (Kano et al., 1984). Kano helps prioritize features that go beyond functionality to enhance satisfaction (Fig. 6.1).

Kansei Engineering, pioneered by Mitsuo Nagamachi (1995), translates desired emotions into design parameters—capturing how users want to feel and embedding those affective qualities into form, texture, feedback, and function. Automotive teams, for example, may translate "sportiness" or "elegance" into specific materials, control feel, or sound design. Kansei often leverages Kano categorization to prioritize which emotional qualities are must-haves, performance-related, or delight-generating—aligning emotional resonance with strategic differentiation.

Quality Function Deployment (QFD), initiated by Yoji Akao (1990), bridges the voice of the customer and engineering specifications. It maps user needs (WHATs) to product design features (HOWs), making empathy traceable in technical decisions (Fig. 6.2). While QFD focuses on functional requirements, Kansei

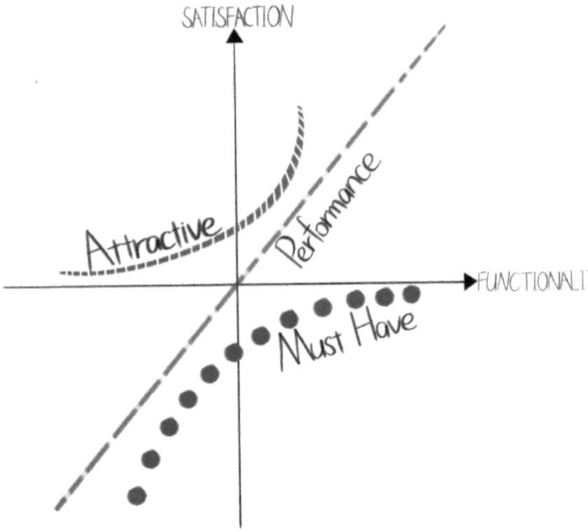

Fig. 6.1 The Kano Model (Kano et al., 1984)

Fig. 6.2 House of quality (Akao, 1990)

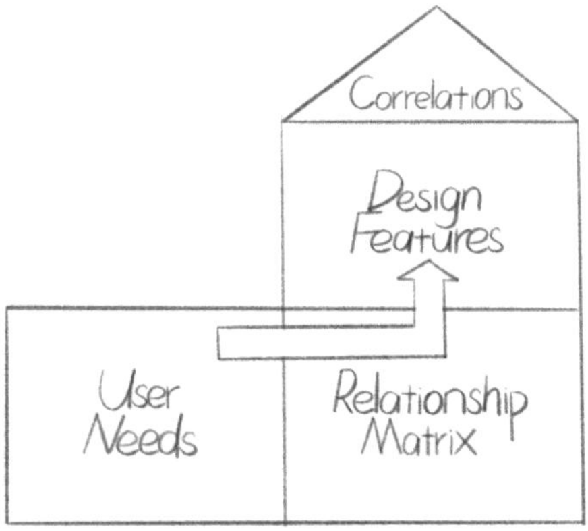

complements it by embedding aesthetic and emotional expectations—together addressing both rational utility and emotional appeal.

Don Norman's book *The Design of Everyday Things* (2013) further clarified UCD via core usability principles—visibility, feedback, affordances, and mappings—rooted in cognitive psychology. Good design "makes the right actions obvious and the wrong actions difficult," producing interfaces that are intuitive and error-resistant.

These frameworks form the backbone of user-centered empathy: actionable, testable, and repeatable. Yet UCD's focus on individual users, while powerful for precision and proximity, risks tunnel vision. It may neglect systemic consequences, collective needs, or long-term impacts. As the scope and responsibility of design expand, a broader paradigm is needed: Human-Centered Design.

Human-Centered Design: Beyond the Individual

Human-Centered Design (HCD) broadens UCD by situating individual users within complex social, cultural, and systemic contexts—socio-technical systems (Buchanan, 2001). Where UCD focuses on direct users and usability, HCD brings attention to deeper values such as dignity, equity, inclusion, and participation. It shifts the central question from "What does the user need?" to "What kind of world are we creating through this design?"

Empathy in HCD is not merely emotional; it is ethical and reflexive. It emphasizes co-creating solutions with diverse stakeholders, including marginalized communities and non-users affected by the system (Manzini, 2015). Participatory design, co-creation workshops, and deliberative processes bring more voices into the design space, allowing empathy to operate at multiple levels: interpersonal, institutional, and systemic.

HCD also invites designers to recognize their own biases and embeddedness. Empathy becomes dialogical—not only seeing others, but also being seen and held accountable. Designers are no longer neutral observers; they are actors shaping outcomes with ethical and social implications. In domains such as healthcare, education, and governance, this reflexive stance is crucial for responsible design.

Cognitively, HCD draws on anthropology, psychology, and systems thinking. It acknowledges the complexity of human behavior, power relations, and the unintended consequences of interventions. By embracing this complexity, HCD supports more adaptive, inclusive, and context-sensitive solutions that transcend the limits of conventional usability.

In short, HCD expands empathy from a technique to a design ethos. It integrates emotional understanding with critical thinking, systemic awareness, and moral deliberation. Empathy becomes both compass and constraint for navigating messy, real-world design challenges.

Humanity-Centered Design: Empathy at Planetary Scale

In recent years, discourse on design empathy has expanded beyond user- and even human-centered paradigms. This evolution is crystallized in Humanity-Centered Design (HuCD), championed by thinkers such as Don Norman in *Design for a Better World* (2023). HuCD asks designers to extend their circle of concern from individuals and communities to humanity, the planet, and future generations (Friedman et al., 2014).

Humanity-Centered Design (HuCD) begins with the recognition that design decisions carry long-term, large-scale consequences. Many contemporary crises—climate change, inequality, digital addiction, unsustainable consumption—partly stem from designs optimized for short-term convenience or gain at the expense of ecological and social sustainability.

At this level, empathy becomes a systems ethic, compelling designers to consider how choices ripple across time, geography, and ecosystems. A smartphone may excel in usability yet fail sustainability if it generates e-waste or exploits labor; a transport app might optimize individual journeys while worsening congestion and emissions. HuCD seeks to move beyond such myopia.

Rather than incremental fixes, HuCD reframes the questions: not just how to design better cars, but how to redesign cities; not how to sell more devices, but how to foster digital well-being; not how to maximize profit, but how to steward planetary resources responsibly (Bhamra & Lofthouse, 2008). It aims for harmony among people, technology, and nature, embedding sustainability, equity, and intergenerational justice as fundamental design criteria.

Importantly, HuCD does not abandon the individual user; it situates personal experience within a broader fabric of collective responsibility and shared futures. Building on the precision of UCD and the ethical sensibility of HCD—while adding a planetary perspective—HuCD redefines empathy as caring not only for immediate user needs but for humanity's long-term survival and flourishing.

Evolution of Design Empathy

Empathy in design has widened from the individual to the systemic and, finally, to the planetary. Rather than replacing one another, these lenses are additive: each new scope retains the previous while expanding responsibility (see Fig. 6.3).

- User-Centered Design (UCD) anchors empathy in usability, satisfaction, and the fit between product and task.
- Human-Centered Design (HCD) extends empathy to the whole person and their context, emphasizing dignity, participation, and systemic well-being.
- Humanity-Centered Design (HuCD) pushes further, embedding empathy for ecosystems, society, and future generations, and advocating responsible, sustainable design at planetary scale.

As empathy scales, so do design criteria and accountability. UCD asks, "Is it usable and valuable to the user?" HCD adds, "Is it equitable and context-appropriate?" HuCD adds, "Is it sustainable and just over time and across systems?" Practically, this means expanding evidence (from user tests to societal and ecological indicators), widening stakeholders (from users to communities and regulators), and lengthening horizons (from immediate launch to lifecycle and legacy).

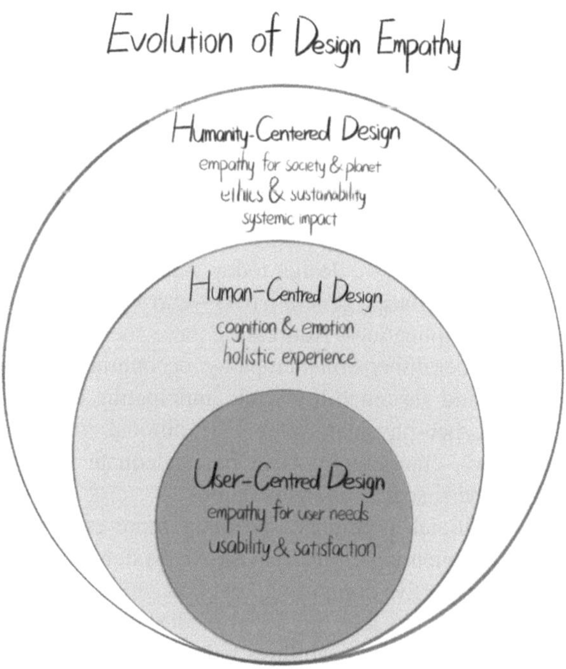

Fig. 6.3 Evolution of design empathy

Empathy as Skill, Process, and Challenge

Empathy in design is not an emotional impulse or a matter of "good intentions." It is a skill that can be cultivated through practice, structure, and humility. Designers often speak of "walking in the user's shoes," but genuine empathic design requires systematic methods for discovering, interpreting, and applying insights about lived realities. Techniques such as in-depth interviews, contextual inquiry, journey mapping, cultural probes, experience prototyping, and participatory workshops provide scaffolds that make empathy actionable.

Even with these tools, empathy is not guaranteed. Teams must guard against empathy theater—performative activities that mimic engagement without producing real understanding or change. Bias, assumption, and projection can distort intent: designers may filter insights through their own worldview, over-identify with familiar groups, or exoticize unfamiliar cultures. Empathy also has limits—no one can fully inhabit another's experience. This makes reflexivity essential: an explicit awareness of one's positionality, blind spots, and interpretive frames.

Design education increasingly treats empathy as a core competency, alongside aesthetics, engineering, and business. Studios, innovation programs, and design schools build it through research practice and through perspective-taking, inclusive storytelling, and ethical foresight. Empathy is taught as both practice and mindset—iterative, humble, and critical. It is not a fixed trait but an ongoing process of listening, questioning, co-creating, and adapting—anchoring design in genuine human connection while acknowledging its limits. True design empathy is not about walking in another's shoes; it is about walking alongside people to shape a better world.

Artificial Empathy: Augmenting Empathy with AI

The technologies we design today—autonomous vehicles, genome editing, brain–computer interfaces, generative AI—carry profound ethical, economic, societal, and systemic implications. Addressing these socio-technical challenges requires higher order, higher dimensional empathy: accounting for values such as equality, justice, privacy, and sustainability while anticipating emergent outcomes across complex human–cyber–physical systems. Traditional empathy-building methods—surveys, interviews, ethnography—can be inadequate when the problem spans multiple stakeholders, scales, and generations.

As artificial intelligence becomes more embedded in practice, a new frontier opens: augmenting empathy with AI. Systems powered by large language models (LLMs), affective computing, and behavioral analytics can process massive datasets—from usage logs to social-media sentiment—and surface patterns humans might miss. These capabilities help designers anticipate frustrations, preferences, and even emotional responses at scale, extending empathic reach.

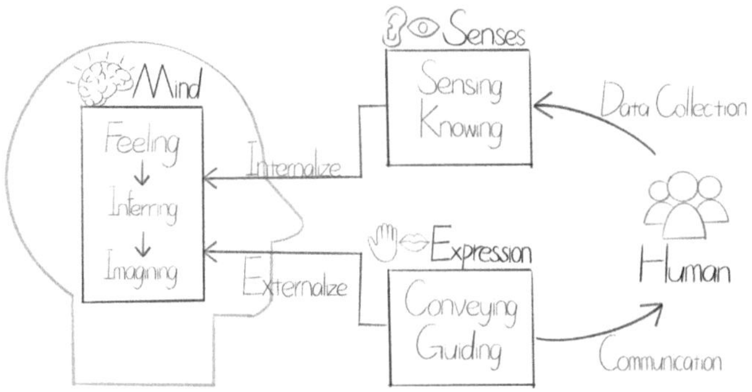

Fig. 6.4 Modules of artificial empathy: senses, mind, and expression (Zhu & Luo, 2024)

Recent work advances the concept of artificial empathy (Zhu & Luo, 2024), which aims to computationally model empathic processes so machines can contribute to Human-Centered Design. Two complementary components are central: affective empathy (recognizing and mirroring emotions) and cognitive empathy (inferring beliefs, intentions, and needs). By decomposing empathy into modules—senses, mind, expression—AI systems can begin to replicate aspects of empathic understanding that designers rely on (Fig. 6.4).

LLMs, in particular, show promise for mental inference—inferring users' underlying goals and psychological needs from unstructured inputs such as reviews or comments. Experiments suggest LLMs can reach empathic accuracy comparable to human designers when mapping statements to motivational goals and needs (Zhu et al., 2025). This points to a potential easing of the classic trade-off between depth (rich insights from few users) and scale (broad but shallow insights): AI may provide more of both.

AI tools are already supporting empathic design. LLM-based co-design agents can generate personas, analyze usability data, simulate conversations, and model user journeys. Sentiment analysis and affective computing detect hidden pain points or emotional patterns in large datasets. Chatbots and voice assistants are increasingly capable of responding with empathy-like behaviors. In these ways, AI functions as an associative engine, extending empathic inquiry and revealing connections beyond any single designer's experience.

Yet computational empathy is double-edged. Machines can mimic the forms of empathy, but can they truly empathize? What is lost when designers outsource empathic work to AI models? Risks include reinforcing bias, flattening cultural nuance, and weakening the relationships at the heart of co-design. The lesson is clear: AI should extend empathy, not replace it.

The promise lies in human–AI empathy partnerships. Used judiciously, AI can amplify understanding, surface hidden insights, and support inclusive design. To realize this potential, deployment must be guided by ethical oversight, cultural sensitivity, and reflexive practice. Empathy in the age of AI becomes a collaborative act—where human judgment, humility, and care remain central, and technology serves as a powerful but bounded ally.

Toward a More Empathic Design Ethos

The evolution of design empathy—from user-centered usability to human-centered dignity to humanity-centered sustainability—reveals a widening horizon of care and responsibility. Empathy has grown from a technique for uncovering needs into a methodological and moral compass for designing in a world marked by ecological fragility, social inequity, and technological disruption. Today, empathy means not only walking in an individual user's shoes, but also recognizing the interdependence of communities, societies, and planetary systems.

At the same time, empathy is a living, evolving practice. It demands humility, reflexivity, and vigilance against bias or superficiality. Emerging AI tools can augment empathic capacity—offering scale and precision that humans alone cannot achieve—but their value lies in extending human judgment, not replacing it: helping designers see further, listen more deeply, and anticipate more responsibly. In this light, design empathy is both skill and ethos—a commitment to design with, for, and ultimately beyond ourselves, in pursuit of a more just, inclusive, and sustainable future.

References

Akao, Y. (1990). *Quality function deployment: Integrating customer requirements into product design*. Productivity Press.

Bhamra, T., & Lofthouse, V. (2008). *Design for Sustainability: A practical approach*. Gower Publishing. – Presents tools and strategies for integrating sustainability into product and systems design.

Buchanan, R. (2001). Human-centered design: A new responsibility for designers in a global context. *Design Issues, 17*(4), 3–8.

Friedman, K., Lou, Y., Norman, D., Stappers, P. J., Voûte, E., & Whitney, P. (2014). *DesignX: A future path for design*. JND.org.

Kano, N., Seraku, N., Takahashi, F., & Tsuji, S. (1984). Attractive quality and must-be quality. *Journal of the Japanese Society for Quality Control, 14*(2), 39–48.

Manzini, E. (2015). *Design, when everybody designs: An introduction to design for social innovation*. The MIT Press.

Nagamachi, M. (1995). Kansei engineering: A new ergonomic consumer-oriented technology for product development. *International Journal of Industrial Ergonomics, 15*(1), 3–11.

Norman, D. A. (2013). *The design of everyday things* (Revised and expanded edition). Basic Books.

Norman, D. A. (2023). *Design for a better world: Meaningful, sustainable, humanity centered*. The MIT Press.

Zhu, Q., & Luo, J. (2024). Artificial empathy: A framework and research agenda for empathic design with artificial intelligence. *Journal of Mechanical Design, 146*(6), 061401.

Zhu, Q., Chong, L., Yang, M. C., & Luo, J. (2025). Reading users' minds with large language models: Mental inference for artificial empathy in design. *Journal of Mechanical Design, 147*(6), 061401.

Chapter 7
Design Heuristics

Abstract Heuristics are fast-and-frugal strategies that guide action under uncertainty. We define what design heuristics are, why they matter under bounded rationality, and how they operate from framing through ideation to evaluation. A practical typology—form-, function-, behavior-, and system-based heuristics—helps designers move from open exploration to focused progress. The chapter also shows how to build an "adaptive toolbox" and demonstrates reflective use: naming, testing, refining, and combining heuristics with analysis.

What Are Design Heuristics

Design rarely proceeds by fixed procedures for well-defined problems. It unfolds amid ambiguity, novelty, and change—incomplete information, shifting constraints, evolving needs. Under such conditions, rigid rules and exhaustive computation often fall short. Designers instead lean on heuristics: informal, experience-based strategies that generate options and steer choices when certainty is scarce.

Heuristics are more than shortcuts. They are cognitive moves and generative principles that help transform what we know into what might be. They do not guarantee optimality, but they enable timely, effective action by opening promising directions, structuring exploration, and focusing evaluation. In practice, design heuristics tend to:

- Span levels: from framing problems to generating concepts to pruning options
- Favor progress over perfection: trading exhaustive search for workable advances
- Leverage precedent: reusing patterns, analogies, and rules-of-thumb to navigate uncertainty
- Remain teachable: they can be named, practiced, critiqued, and refined

Used alongside analysis, heuristics propose and propel—together they allow generative and decisive movement in open-ended spaces where something genuinely new must be created.

J. Luo, *Design Science*, Applied Innovation and Technology Management,
https://doi.org/10.1007/978-3-032-13353-3_7

Why Heuristics Matter in Design

Rooted in cognitive psychology and decision science—most notably the work of Herbert Simon and Gerd Gigerenzer—heuristics are central to bounded rationality, the idea that human decision-making is limited by time, knowledge, and cognitive capacity (Simon, 1996). These limits are not flaws; they are the context in which heuristics excel—delivering good-enough solutions quickly when perfection is neither feasible nor necessary.

In design, heuristics are not only decision aids but generative principles. They frame problem spaces, suggest transformations and analogies, prompt exploration, and open diverse paths to solutions. For example: "break it into modules" can unlock new architectures; "reuse existing components" can speed iteration and reduce cost; "design for failure" guides robustness under uncertainty. These are not formulas but lightweight, flexible tools.

Gigerenzer's adaptive toolbox argues that human cognition excels when equipped with a repertoire of situation-specific heuristics (Gigerenzer, 2001). Unlike "unbounded" rationality—which assumes unlimited computation and perfect information—the toolbox view embraces real constraints and shows how simple, fast, and frugal heuristics can outperform optimization under uncertainty (Fig. 7.1).

This is especially relevant in design, where decisions are often made under time pressure, incomplete data, and shifting goals. Fast and frugal heuristics do not bypass thinking—they structure it. They help designers make context-sensitive judgments, reduce cognitive load, act decisively, and stay open to iteration. Rather than constraining creativity, heuristics fuel it: they scaffold ideation, support rapid prototyping, and enable iterative learning. Many breakthroughs arise not from rigid methods but from skillful, context-aware use of heuristics.

Design routinely tackles wicked problems—ambiguous objectives, evolving constraints, no single "right" answer. Heuristics offer a way to navigate complexity without paralysis: moving from vague intentions to tangible artifacts, from open-ended exploration to informed experimentation. Used reflectively and adaptively, they transform ambiguity into insight—and insight into impactful solutions.

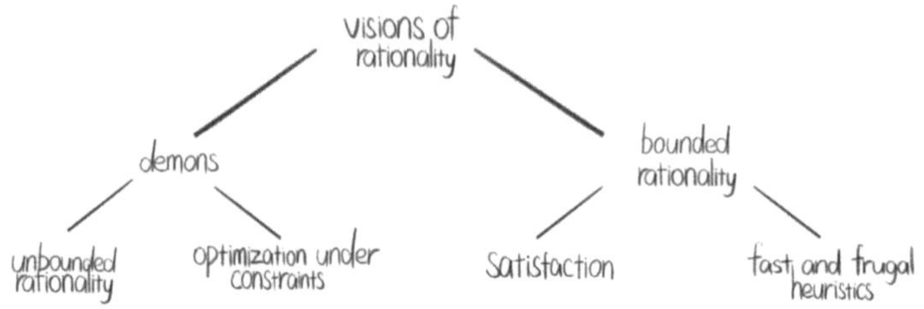

Fig. 7.1 Heuristics in models of rationality (Gigerenzer, 2001)

Categories of Design Heuristics

Design heuristics range from broad, domain-agnostic ideation strategies to task-specific rules. Some ignite early exploration; others support refinement and system-level integration. Together they form an adaptive cognitive toolkit for navigating ambiguity and complexity in the design process.

Across design practice and education, several domain-agnostic ideation heuristics (Fig. 7.2) consistently stand out for versatility and generative power. These high-level heuristics are cognitively potent. Heuristics like combine and analogy help break entrenched patterns, recombine existing ideas in novel ways, and synthesize across disciplines.

- Analogy: draw inspiration from unrelated domains—nature, culture, technology—to spark new frames
- Combine: merge existing elements or functions to produce novel configurations
- Substitute: swap an element to shift function, appearance, or performance
- Eliminate: remove components to simplify, reduce cost, or surface latent value
- Reverse: invert roles, positions, or processes to challenge assumptions and reveal unconventional solutions

Often introduced via ideation frameworks such as SCAMPER (Eberle, 1997), TRIZ (Altshuller, 1999), or biomimicry (Benyus, 1997), these heuristics trigger divergent thinking. Their simplicity makes them accessible to novice designers, while their flexibility keeps them useful for experts seeking to disrupt conventions, explore alternatives, and build momentum through rapid variation and low-cost experimentation.

As problems become more defined and solutions more refined, designers benefit from targeted heuristics keyed to the task at hand—shaping form, defining function, orchestrating interaction, or managing systemic complexity. A practical typology groups heuristics by the primary design dimension they address:

Fig. 7.2 Common heuristics used in early-phase design ideation

- Form-based—physical shape, aesthetics, and layout
- Function-based—capabilities, operations, and purpose
- Behavior-based—interactions among users, systems, and environments
- System-based—complexity, modularity, and interdependencies

This structured lens clarifies how heuristics operate across abstraction levels—from surface aesthetics to deep system logic. So, designers can apply them with strategic intent—whether to inspire form, improve usability, optimize systems, or enhance functionality. The following sections elaborate on each category in turn.

Form-Based Heuristics

Form-based heuristics guide the manipulation of an artifact's physical appearance, spatial configuration, or visual expression. These heuristics often operate at the intersection of aesthetics, usability, and branding, shaping how users perceive and engage with a product. Some examples:

- Combine or separate: merge related elements into a cohesive whole or divide a complex object into manageable modules to enhance clarity, flexibility, or customization.
- Mirror or rotate: use symmetry to suggest balance and harmony, or introduce asymmetry for novelty and distinctiveness.
- Enlarge or shrink: adjust dimensions to optimize ergonomics, signal importance, or adapt to constraints in the environment.
- Repeat or vary: introduce patterns for familiarity or deliberate variation to draw attention and sustain user engagement.

Such heuristics are particularly prominent in industrial design, architecture, and interface layout, where form directly affects human perception and experience. They help designers explore visual rhythm, spatial harmony, and sensory feedback while supporting material feasibility and manufacturability.

Function-Based Heuristics

Function-based heuristics focus on what the design does—its operational purpose, capability set, and intended utility. These heuristics are especially valuable during concept generation and redesign phases, when exploring alternative uses, improving functionality, or adapting to emerging needs. For example:

- Add or eliminate functions: introduce new features to increase versatility or strip away non-essentials to streamline usability and cost.
- Change the sequence: reorder operational steps or user flows to improve intuitiveness, efficiency, or safety.

- Enable multi-functionality: design components to serve multiple roles, reducing part count and enhancing space or weight efficiency.
- Reframe purpose: rethink the core objective of the product or system, often sparking novel applications or pivoting the value proposition.

These heuristics promote functional innovation by challenging default assumptions and reframing the problem, enabling designers to uncover latent needs or previously unconsidered opportunities.

Behavior-Based Heuristics

Behavior-based heuristics address how a product or system behaves in interaction with its users or environment. These heuristics are fundamental to human-centered and interaction design, ensuring that the artifact supports intuitive, safe, and satisfying user experiences. For example:

- Trigger with feedback: provide immediate, understandable responses to user inputs, closing the action-perception loop.
- Delay or accelerate action: modulate the timing of operations to align with human rhythms, expectations, or safety thresholds.
- Allow learning and adaptation: enable products to evolve with user proficiency or preferences, supporting personalization and long-term satisfaction.
- Switch modes automatically: allow the system to detect and respond to contextual changes—such as ambient light, user state, or environment to enhance utility and convenience.

These heuristics align design decisions with cognitive and perceptual characteristics, promoting usability, accessibility, and emotional engagement. They are particularly relevant in software UX, consumer electronics, services, and assistive technologies.

System-Based Heuristics

System-based heuristics enable designers to manage complexity across interconnected components, subsystems, or socio-technical environments. They are crucial when designing products embedded within larger operational, ecological, or organizational systems. For example:

- Decouple or isolate subsystems: prevent cascading failures by creating modular boundaries and localized control.
- Standardize interfaces: facilitate interchangeability, upgrades, and collaboration across teams or organizations.

- Embed feedback loops: integrate sensors or user data collection mechanisms to enable learning, monitoring, and real-time adaptation.
- Optimize at system level: balance performance across the entire system rather than optimizing individual components in isolation.

These heuristics support holistic thinking by encouraging attention to emergent behavior, interoperability, resilience, and long-term adaptability. They are widely used in engineering systems, infrastructure design, and complex product-service ecosystems.

Together, this typology prepares the ground for applying heuristics with purpose: inspire form, enhance function, improve interaction, and stabilize systems—all while keeping exploration fast, frugal, and focused.

Origins of Design Heuristics

Design heuristics do not emerge from a single source; they evolve from diverse origins that reflect both the rigor and creativity of the design process. Understanding where heuristics come from helps illuminate how they function as both cognitive tools and cultural knowledge.

Personal Experience

Many heuristics are rooted in individual practice. Through cycles of trial and error, reflection, and learning from failure, designers internalize strategies that have proven effective in past projects. Over time, these experiences solidify into intuitive rules—what Donald Schön (1983) calls "knowing-in-action"—that guide future decisions. For example, a designer who has repeatedly encountered failure when overcomplicating user interfaces may adopt a personal heuristic such as "eliminate one feature from every prototype."

Disciplinary Knowledge

Some heuristics are institutionalized within specific fields. Engineering disciplines, for example, rely on time-tested design principles like "fail-safe design" or "minimize tolerance stack-up" that are passed down through textbooks and training. In architecture, "form follows function" is a foundational heuristic. In human-computer interaction, heuristics such as "recognition over recall" from Nielsen (1994)'s usability heuristics shape the way interfaces are evaluated and improved. These heuristics reflect a body of codified wisdom shared within a design community.

Analogical Transfer

Designers are natural analogical thinkers. They often borrow solutions from nature (biomimicry), art, or other domains to inspire innovation. For instance, Velcro was invented after observing how burrs stick to dog fur—an example of analogical transfer from biology. Artists' use of contrast or negative space might inspire heuristics in information design or branding. This cross-domain borrowing expands the creative repertoire of designers beyond the limits of their primary field.

Empirical Studies

Design researchers have systematically elicited and codified heuristics through empirical observation. The Design Heuristics Project (Yilmaz & Seifert, 2011), for example, developed a set of 77 heuristics based on analyzing award-winning product designs and observing design students' ideation behaviors. These empirically grounded heuristics serve as ideation tools to spark novel solutions and broaden a designer's creative space.

While some heuristics are explicitly taught in classrooms or encoded in design toolkits, many remain tacit—embedded in the practices, habits, and intuitions of experienced designers. These unwritten rules are passed down through mentorship, studio critique, and practice, rather than formal instruction. In this way, design heuristics represent both personal craftsmanship and collective intelligence, evolving through communities of practice as well as individual insight.

Heuristics in Practice

In real-world design practice, heuristics are not rigid formulas or mechanical checklists. Instead, they function more like a seasoned chef's intuition—tools that experienced designers draw upon, combine, adapt, and occasionally override depending on the unique demands of a project (Lawson, 2006). Far from following any single rule rigidly, expert designers engage with heuristics as a flexible and situational resource—a cognitive toolkit that grows with experience.

For instance, in the high-velocity environment of a startup, where uncertainty is high and resources are limited, a team might embrace the heuristic of "build fast, fail faster" or "rapid prototyping" to quickly test user reactions to multiple MVPs (minimum viable products). This approach minimizes the cost of failure while accelerating learning, helping the team iterate toward product-market fit.

In contrast, a car manufacturer tackling the design of a new vehicle platform may lean on more structured and cost-sensitive heuristics such as "maximize modularity" or "reuse existing components." These principles help manage complexity, reduce production costs, and shorten development cycles—all critical in highly regulated and capital-intensive industries.

In digital interface design, widely accepted heuristics like "keep it simple" and "show what's next" guide decisions about screen layouts, interaction flows, and user onboarding. These heuristics help designers reduce cognitive load and support intuitive user experiences—especially crucial in mobile apps and web-based tools where user attention is fleeting.

Heuristics also encourage cross-pollination across domains. Consider the biomimetic insight that "form follows function"—observed in bird wings optimized for flight—which has inspired aerodynamic shaping in drone and aircraft design. Similarly, fractal patterns found in nature have influenced architectural structures and materials science, while musical rhythm has informed design approaches to pacing and sequencing in user experience flows.

Ultimately, heuristics serve as bridges between insight and action. They make abstract principles usable, enabling designers to navigate ambiguity, generate alternatives, and make decisions with incomplete information. Mastery of heuristics is not about memorizing rules but about developing the judgment to deploy them effectively—recognizing which to use, when to apply them, and when to break them.

As such, heuristics empower designers to adapt, improvise, and innovate—qualities essential not only for solving well-defined problems but also for tackling the open-ended challenges that define ambitious, real-world design.

Heuristics and Creativity

Heuristics enable creativity. They help designers break through the paralysis of a blank slate by framing the problem space and suggesting productive directions for exploration. In this sense, they act as creative catalysts: sparking variation, prompting ideation, and offering generative starting points from which entirely new concepts can emerge. By offering a "way in" to complex or ill-defined challenges, heuristics unlock creative momentum.

Moreover, heuristics play a crucial role in iterative learning. They encourage low-cost experimentation and fast feedback, which are essential for adaptive design. When applied with flexibility, heuristics enable designers to fail fast, learn quickly, and iterate effectively—a cycle central to both innovation and design thinking. Whether sketching early concepts or refining system architectures, heuristics help make ambiguity more actionable.

However, heuristics are not infallible. When used dogmatically or without reflection, they can inadvertently constrain creativity, anchoring designers to familiar solutions or preventing exploration of alternative paths. The risk is not in the heuristics themselves, but in treating them as fixed rules rather than flexible tools. Like any design method, heuristics must be applied with judgment.

This brings us to the notion of heuristic literacy—the ability to choose, adapt, and even invent heuristics strategically. Just as process literacy enables designers to navigate between different design process models, heuristic literacy empowers them to apply generative principles with awareness and agility. Reflective practitioners develop an intuitive sense of when to apply a heuristic and when to discard it, how to balance multiple heuristics in tension—such as "keep it simple" versus "make it multifunctional," and how to generate new heuristics from personal experience, user feedback, or interdisciplinary insights.

Building such literacy requires exposure, practice, and mentorship. Educators play a vital role in cultivating heuristic fluency—not by prescribing a fixed set of design rules, but by modeling how heuristics are used in practice: when to follow them, how to adapt them, and how to question them. Studio critiques, case studies, and design journals offer fertile ground for helping students surface their own implicit heuristics and sharpen their judgment over time.

Ultimately, design heuristics are tools for thinking—not shortcuts to solutions. They help designers navigate the uncertain, the ambiguous, and the emergent. But like any tools, their value lies in how they are wielded. Used reflexively and strategically, heuristics empower designers not just to solve problems, but to reframe them—and in doing so, to innovate.

Heuristics as a Language of Design

Design heuristics are indispensable cognitive tools that empower designers to navigate complexity, embrace ambiguity, and foster creativity. They strike a productive balance between structure and flexibility—providing enough guidance to focus exploration, while leaving room for surprise. Unlike rigid procedures, heuristics serve as generative prompts that support designers in making sense of messy, ill-defined problems and in moving fluidly between ideation, iteration, and implementation.

Across different layers of design—form, function, behavior, and system—heuristics help translate abstract intentions into tangible and impactful outcomes. They support critical tasks such as identifying user needs, generating alternative solutions, making informed trade-offs, and adapting to shifting constraints or feedback. In doing so, heuristics become a language of design—one that blends intuition, experience, and knowledge to turn vision into reality.

Ultimately, mastery of design heuristics is not about memorizing a fixed set of rules, but about developing the sensitivity to choose, adapt, and invent them as situations demand. They are not merely shortcuts—they are scaffolds for creative thinking, decision-making, and problem-solving in a world where uncertainty is the norm. As such, heuristics are central not only to effective design practice but also to the evolution of design as a discipline.

References

Altshuller, G. (1999). *The innovation algorithm: TRIZ, Systematic Innovation and Technical Creativity*. Technical Innovation Center.

Benyus, J. M. (1997). *Biomimicry: Innovation inspired by nature*. William Morrow.

Eberle, B. (1997). *SCAMPER: Creative games and activities for imagination development*. D.O.K. Publishers.

Gigerenzer, G. (2001). The adaptive toolbox. In G. Gigerenzer & R. Selten (Eds.), *Bounded rationality: The adaptive toolbox* (pp. 37–50). MIT Press.

Lawson, B. (2006). *How designers think: The design process demystified* (4th ed.). Architectural Press.

Nielsen, J. (1994). *Usability engineering*. Morgan Kaufmann.

Schön, D. A. (1983). *The reflective practitioner: How professionals think in action*. Basic Books.

Simon, H. A. (1996). *The sciences of the artificial* (3rd ed.). MIT Press.

Yilmaz, S., & Seifert, C. M. (2011). Design heuristics for idea generation. *Design Studies, 32*(6), 623–647.

Chapter 8
Design Prototyping

Abstract Prototyping turns speculation into evidence. We map modalities—physical, digital, service, and experience prototypes—and show how to choose the right fidelity to answer the next question fast. Craftsmanship is foregrounded: sketching, building, instrumenting, and refining in contact with materials, users, and constraints. With examples from additive-manufacturing-enabled iteration and data-rich testing, the chapter frames prototypes as boundary objects that align stakeholders, de-risk decisions, and accelerate learning.

What Is Prototyping

Prototyping is a cornerstone of design practice and innovation. At its essence, prototyping is the act of giving form—physical, digital, or experiential—to an idea so that it can be explored, tested, and refined. It foregrounds craftsmanship—the hands-on skills, material fluency, and disciplined build-measure habits that turn ideas into evidence.

A prototype is not merely an object but a vehicle for learning—a tangible or virtual representation of critical aspects of an intended concept, built not to be perfect, but to make ideas concrete enough to interrogate and improve. Prototypes take many shapes—from paper sketches and cardboard models to interface wireframe and role-played services. What unites these diverse expressions is a shared purpose: to bridge imagination and reality by creating something that can be engaged with, critiqued, and evolved.

Prototyping reframes the act of design from speculation to experimentation. Prototypes are not miniature versions of the final products. Instead, they are boundary objects that allow designers, users, and stakeholders to converse about what could be (Houde & Hill, 1997). A sketch externalizes an idea for questioning; a mock-up invites discussion of scale and ergonomics; a simulation surfaces usability issues before code is written. By embodying abstractions in testable forms, prototypes create fast feedback, iteration, and collective sensemaking. In this way, prototyping is not just a step in the design process, but a way of thinking.

J. Luo, *Design Science*, Applied Innovation and Technology Management,
https://doi.org/10.1007/978-3-032-13353-3_8

Roles of Prototyping

Prototyping transforms uncertainty into insight. It is learning-by-making—using tangible experiments to ask questions that speculation cannot answer. Each prototype provides a feedback loop that enables designers to surface blind spots, uncover assumptions, and incrementally improve ideas. It allows failures to occur early, cheaply, and informatively, before they become costly mistakes later in development. In this way, prototyping is not just a way to test ideas but a way to think through making, advancing understanding step by step (Camburn et al., 2017). Figure 8.1 summarizes these roles of prototyping.

Beyond learning, prototyping serves as a critical medium of communication and collaboration. Even a sketch or mock-up can provide a common reference point for discussion among diverse stakeholders, reducing ambiguity and aligning perspectives (Lauff et al., 2020). Prototypes also enable exploration, helping designers generate new concepts, discover unexpected opportunities, and push beyond conventional thinking. Prototypes expand the design space by allowing partial, situated explorations of functionality, interaction, and experience. In this sense, prototypes are not only vehicles for validation but also catalysts for creativity.

Finally, prototyping plays a role in knowledge creation. The act of building and testing prototypes produces new understanding about both the artifact being designed and the broader phenomena it interacts with. Whether probing user behavior, material properties, or system dynamics, prototypes help generate design knowledge that endures beyond a single project. Thus, prototyping is central not only to developing better products and systems but also to advancing design as a discipline.

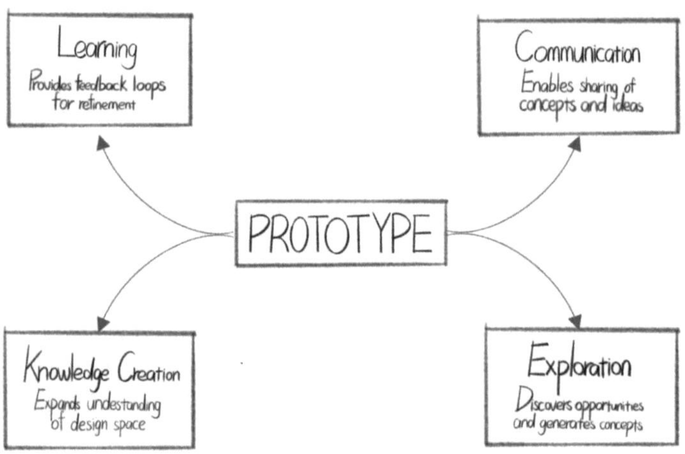

Fig. 8.1 Roles of prototyping

When to Prototype

The guiding mantra of modern design practice is: prototype early and prototype often. Waiting until the end of a project to test ideas risks catastrophic failure when changes are most expensive (Ulrich & Eppinger, 2015). By contrast, early prototypes expose blind spots, reveal hidden assumptions, and invite user reactions at a stage when revisions are relatively easy. They allow designers to front-load learning, shifting uncertainty from late-stage deployment to early exploration, where it is less costly and more generative (Otto & Wood, 2001).

Prototyping is not a one-time checkpoint but an iterative cycle woven throughout the design process. Each round of making and testing informs the next, enabling designers to refine concepts, pivot directions, or even reframe the problem itself. Iterative prototyping accelerates design learning by creating a rhythm of hypothesis, experiment, and reflection. In early stages, quick and rough prototypes help explore possibilities and stimulate imagination. As the design matures, higher fidelity prototypes allow for rigorous testing of functionality, usability, and performance.

Importantly, prototyping should be viewed not as a discrete phase but as a continuous practice. Prototypes can appear at the fuzzy front end of innovation to spark ideation, in the middle to converge on feasible solutions, and at the end to validate designs in real-world conditions. Whether used to provoke, to explore, or to confirm, prototypes are the heartbeat of iterative design—a tool for learning at every stage.

Fidelities of Prototypes

Prototypes exist along a spectrum of fidelity, ranging from quick sketches to fully functional models. Fidelity refers to the level of detail, realism, and completeness with which a prototype represents the envisioned product, system, or service in form, function, and interaction. Choosing the right fidelity is not a matter of better or worse, but of purpose: the appropriate fidelity is the one that best serves the questions being asked at that stage of the design process (Lim et al., 2008).

Low-fidelity prototypes include sketches, paper interfaces, cardboard mock-ups, or simple role-plays. Their power lies in their speed and disposability: because they are quick and inexpensive to produce, they invite bold exploration and fearless iteration (Yang, 2005). Low-fidelity artifacts also encourage honest feedback—users feel free to critique something clearly unfinished in ways they may hesitate to with polished models (Fig. 8.2).

Medium-fidelity prototypes capture more detail and allow for deeper exploration. These may include interactive wireframes, digital mock-ups, partial physical models, or click-through app prototypes. At this stage, designers can test flows, interactions, or ergonomics, and begin to evaluate how ideas might perform in more realistic conditions without committing the resources required for high-fidelity development.

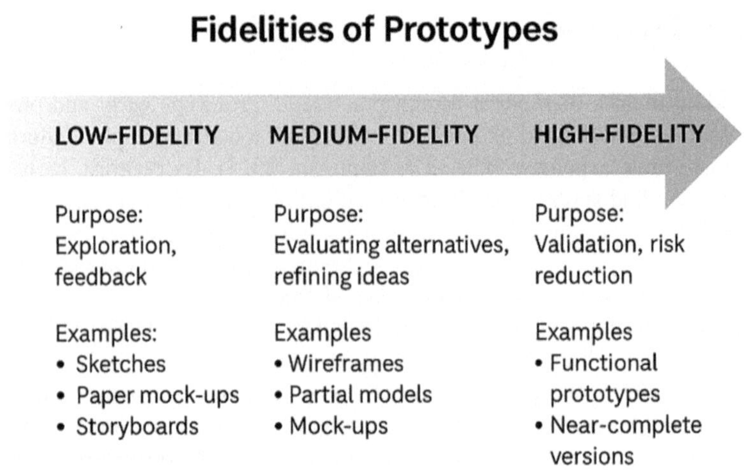

Fig. 8.2 Fidelities of prototypes

High-fidelity prototypes resemble the final product in both look and function. They may be fully engineered testbeds, advanced digital simulations, or refined service enactments. High-fidelity prototypes are used to evaluate performance, build trust with stakeholders, and simulate real-world conditions. Their polish makes them useful for persuasion and validation, though their cost and time intensiveness make them less suitable for early exploration.

Importantly, even the simplest sketch or storyboard can serve as a prototype—not as an artistic rendering but as a thinking tool. By externalizing abstract ideas into tangible form, sketches, diagrams, and storyboards enable rapid communication, creative reflection, and shared understanding.

The art of prototyping lies not in always striving for higher fidelity, but in deliberately matching fidelity to purpose (Yang, 2005). Early ideation thrives on roughness and speed, while later validation demands detail and precision. Moving fluidly along this spectrum allows teams to explore widely, converge thoughtfully, and build confidence step by step.

Modalities of Prototypes

Prototyping is not limited to physical artifacts; it encompasses a wide spectrum of modalities that allow designers to explore, test, and communicate ideas across different domains of interaction. Each modality provides unique insights, and together they reflect the breadth of design practice—from tangible products to intangible services and experiences (Lim et al., 2008) (Table 8.1).

Physical prototypes are the most traditional and intuitive forms—mock-ups, scale models, 3D prints, and mechanical assemblies that bring ideas into the material world. They allow designers to assess ergonomics, manufacturability, and performance while revealing actual in-hand behavior. A quick cardboard model, for

Table 8.1 Modalities of prototypes

Modality	Primary focus	Typical examples
Physical	Artifacts & mechanics	Scaled models, 3D prints, assemblies
Digital	Usability & flow	Computer-Aided Design (CAD), Augmented Reality (AR) / Virtual Reality (VR), wireframes, mock-ups
Service	Interactions & processes	Role-play, staged service trials
Experience	Emotions & context	Immersive simulations, contextual tests

example, can settle footprint, grip, and reach before committing to tooling. Building on that speed, additive manufacturing (AM) extends physical prototyping with rapid, low-tooling iterations and supports geometric complexity (e.g., internal channels, lattices), enabling designers to probe form, fitness, and early manufacturability in parallel (Gibson et al., 2021).

In software and interactive systems, digital prototypes—wireframes, clickable mock-ups, or AR/VR simulations—allow designers to simulate interactions, navigation flows, and feedback loops before committing to code. They support rapid iteration across levels of fidelity, from sketchy concepts to data-driven simulations, so stakeholders can experience tasks, states, and edge cases—and align on information architecture and responsiveness—before a single line of production code is written. Because they are quick to revise and easy to instrument for usability evidence, digital prototyping has become a cornerstone of user experience (UX) and service design.

Beyond UX, for complex engineered products, high-fidelity computer-aided design (CAD) models and validated physics-based simulation often yields more accurate, earlier and cheaper decision-grade evidence than physical builds whose accuracy depends on expensive, long-lead tooling. When the governing physics and manufacturing parameters are well characterized, simulation can be the primary test; physical rigs then serve to calibrate and validate models and to exercise integration. The rule of thumb is to choose the cheapest representation that preserves the governing physics and escalate fidelity only as decisions demand.

Service prototypes demostrate that services can—and should—be prototyped. These often take the form of role-playing, "Wizard of Oz" setups, and staged interactions where staff or participants enact end-to-end service flows to surface hidden assumptions and opportunities. A classic example is McDonald's early mock-up of its "Speedee Service System," where employees rehearsed kitchen and customer interactions in a staged environment before committing to large-scale rollout. Such enactments, often paired with service blueprints, props, and timed scripts, help expose friction points in logistics, handoffs, and pacing, and reveal moments that delight or confuse customers.

Experience prototypes simulate how people will feel and behave when interacting with a system in its real-world context. These immersive prototypes are not just about function but about evoking emotion, engagement, and meaning across time. For instance, designers might use VR to simulate the stress of navigating a hospital as a patient, or design a mock environment to recreate the ambience of a future retail concept. By revealing moments of delight, confusion, or anxiety—and how they unfold across touchpoints—experience prototypes align stakeholders on the holistic impact of a design and sharpen decisions about what to build, refine, or remove.

Taken together, these modalities underscore that prototyping is not one-size-fits-all. Physical models highlight mechanics, digital ones surface usability flows, service prototypes uncover human dynamics, and experience prototypes bring forward emotional resonance. By combining modalities, designers build a more complete picture—testing not only how a design works, but also how it feels, scales, and lives in context.

Pretotyping: Faking It Before Making It

Pretotyping, a term popularized by Alberto Savoia, shifts the focus from building things right to first ensuring we are building the right things (Savoia, 2019). Before time, money, and effort are invested into fully fledged prototypes or MVPs, pretotyping offers an ultra-lightweight, low-cost way to test whether a concept resonates with real users and markets. Its mantra—"fake it before you make it"—captures the essence of this strategy: quickly simulate the experience of a product or service to gauge genuine user interest, without committing to full development.

Savoia illustrates this with classic stories: IBM's speech-to-text experiment, where a hidden human typist simulated a voice-recognition system to reveal that people quickly tired of speaking to their computers; and Jeff Hawkins' Palm Pilot wood block, where he carried a piece of wood in his pocket, role-playing its use, to confirm the desirability of a handheld organizer before investing in technology development. These pretotypes revealed crucial insights without building a functional prototype—allowing failure to happen early, cheaply, and informatively.

Pretotypes may take many forms:

- Fake door: a button, webpage, or ad for a product or feature that does not yet exist, to test initial user interest.
- Wizard of Oz/Mechanical Turk: humans secretly perform functions that technology would eventually automate (e.g., IBM's typist simulating speech-to-text).
- Pinocchio: non-functional artifacts that test form, size, or portability (e.g., Hawkins' wood block "Palm Pilot").
- Role-playing services: acting out proposed service flows with staff or users before building infrastructure.
- Provincial: testing ideas in a small market before scaling up.

The power of pretotyping lies in its speed and economy. By stripping away technical polish and focusing purely on desirability, it helps teams answer the most fundamental question: Should we build this at all? In this sense, pretotyping acts as a form of experience prototyping, enabling designers to capture authentic user reactions in highly engaging, real-world contexts without the burden of working technology.

Far from being a shortcut, pretotyping is a discipline of disciplined experimentation. It reduces the risk of overinvesting in ideas that users do not actually want and builds confidence in pursuing concepts that do spark genuine engagement. In the broader continuum of design experimentation, pretotyping represents the earliest, leanest point—a way of putting bold ideas in front of people fast enough to learn what only reality can teach.

Minimum Viable Product (MVP): Learning in the Market

If pretotyping asks "Should we build it at all?," the minimum viable product (MVP) asks "How will it perform in the real world?" Rooted in lean startup methodology (Ries, 2011), the MVP represents the leanest version of a real product that can be deployed to customers. Unlike a pretotype, which fakes or simulates, an MVP is a functioning artifact—but stripped to its bare essentials. It includes only the features necessary to test the core assumptions behind the product's value proposition, usability, and demand.

The MVP is embedded in the build-measure-learn loop, the iterative cycle at the heart of lean startup thinking. Designers and entrepreneurs build a minimal version of the product, release it to a small set of early adopters, gather data on real usage and feedback, and then decide whether to persevere, pivot, or abandon the idea. This disciplined cycle avoids the costly mistake of overbuilding before market fit is proven.

Classic cases illustrate the power of MVP thinking. Dropbox, for instance, famously validated demand through a simple demo video—showing users what the product would do before it existed in full. The overwhelming response from sign-ups provided enough evidence to invest in full development. Similarly, Zappos began with an MVP that was deceptively simple: the founder photographed shoes from local stores, posted them online, and personally fulfilled orders by buying the shoes after customers purchased them. This low-cost experiment validated the viability of online shoe retail before large-scale infrastructure was built.

The MVP sits further along the continuum of experimentation than pretotype or low-fidelity prototypes. It is closer to market reality and thus riskier and more resource-intensive—but also more revealing. An MVP does not aim for perfection; rather, it is deliberately "minimum" to accelerate validated learning. In this sense, MVPs are not the end of the design process, but checkpoints that inform whether to scale, adjust, or stop altogether.

Ultimately, the MVP embodies the spirit of learning in the market—where the real test of a design is not only what users say they want, but how they actually behave when presented with a working product.

From Pretotypes to Prototypes to MVPs: A Continuum of Experimentation

Seen together, pretotyping, prototyping, and MVPs form a continuum of experimentation rather than isolated practices. Each addresses a distinct layer of uncertainty—desirability, feasibility, and viability—while differing in cost, speed, and depth of insight (Fig. 8.3).

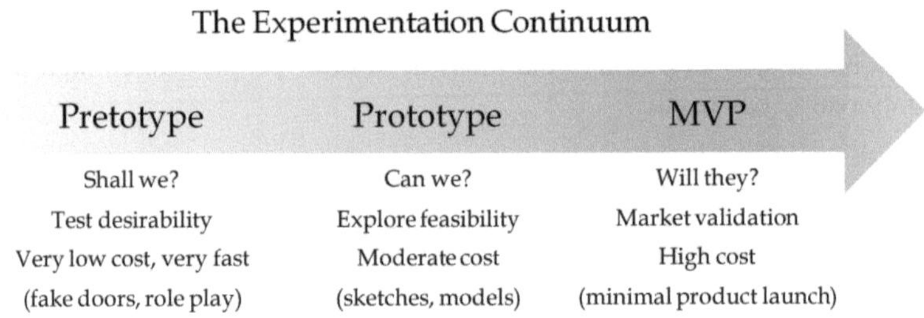

Fig. 8.3 The experimentation continuum: from pretotype to prototype to MVP

Pretotyping asks the most fundamental question: Should this idea exist at all? It relies on quick, low-cost experiments to gauge authentic interest before significant resources are committed. Prototyping then takes promising ideas forward, asking: How might this idea actually work? By making concepts tangible and testable, prototypes enable iteration on form, function, and user experience. Finally, the MVP brings an idea into the marketplace, posing the ultimate test: Will people adopt and pay for this in reality? Though more resource-intensive, MVPs generate the richest feedback because they are validated in real-world conditions.

This progression is best understood not as a rigid pipeline but as a flexible design philosophy. Teams often cycle back and forth: insights from an MVP may prompt fresh pretotypes to explore new directions, while feedback from prototypes may lead to discarding or reframing the idea entirely. What unites all three is a shared ethos: to reduce uncertainty, accelerate learning, and ground innovation in evidence rather than assumption. Taken together, they function as a ladder of experimentation, enabling designers to move systematically from early exploration to market validation.

By mastering when and how to deploy pretotypes, prototypes, and MVPs, teams can de-risk innovation while keeping creativity alive. Pretotypes test desirability, prototypes probe feasibility, and MVPs validate viability. In combination, they create a disciplined yet flexible framework that minimizes waste, amplifies learning, and fosters a culture where bold ideas are explored responsibly and with empathy for users, stakeholders, and society at large (Table 8.2).

Strategic Mindsets for Prototyping

Prototyping is not only a set of tools but also a way of thinking. Its effectiveness depends less on the fidelity of the models than on the mentality with which they are created and used. At its core, prototyping embodies the belief that progress in design comes not from speculation, but from action, feedback, and iteration. This requires cultivating certain mindsets that guide how and why prototypes, pretotypes, and MVPs are deployed. In practice, that mindset is realized as craftsmanship: the disciplined doing that converts speculation into testable form.

Table 8.2 Comparison of pretotyping, prototyping, and MVP

Dimensions	Pretotyping	Prototyping	Minimum viable product
Purpose	Test if the idea is worth pursuing ("build the right it")	Explore and refine how the idea works ("build it right")	Validate value proposition and product–market fit
Form	Fake doors, role-plays, Wizard of Oz, quick hacks	Sketches, mock-ups, 3D models, wireframes, service simulations	Simplified but functional product released to real users
Fidelity	Very low, often illusionary	Low to high, depending on stage	Medium—only core features built
Cost & speed	Extremely low cost; very fast	Moderate cost; time varies with fidelity	Higher cost; requires actual development
Context of use	Simulated or staged settings to provoke real reactions	Controlled settings for testing mechanics, usability, or experience	Real-world environments with early adopters
Insights generated	Gauges initial interest, desirability, and demand	Reveals feasibility, usability, ergonomics, and user interaction patterns	Validates adoption, retention, willingness to pay
Representative example	IBM's fake speech-to-text demo; landing page "fake doors"	IDEO's product mock-ups; McDonald's "Speedee Service System" test	Dropbox's explainer video; Zappos' early shoe sales test
Mentality	"Fail fast, fail cheap"	"Learn by making"	"Build-measure-learn" loop from lean startup

First, designers must embrace a bias toward action. Rather than waiting for per fect information or alignment, effective teams move quickly to externalize ideas. Sketches, mock-ups, or lightweight experiments shift conversations from abstract speculation to tangible possibilities. This goes hand in hand with non-attachment: prototypes are not precious artifacts but disposable learning tools. By treating them as stepping stones rather than finished outcomes, teams remain open to change, iteration, and even radical pivots.

Second, prototyping requires reframing failure as learning. Early iterations will often "fail" in terms of usability, desirability, or technical feasibility, but these failures are not setbacks—they are accelerated feedback loops. Each breakdown illuminates blind spots, helping teams refine ideas and sharpen questions. The guiding principle becomes: fail fast, fail cheaply, and learn deeply. This learning orientation distinguishes innovative cultures from risk-averse ones.

Third, strategic prototyping calls for choosing fidelity deliberately. The right prototype is the one that serves the immediate learning objective. Low-fidelity sketches may be best for exploring many ideas quickly, while high-fidelity models may be needed to inspire stakeholder confidence or test performance in realistic conditions. Pretotypes sit at the extreme low end—where the goal is simply to test demand. MVPs, at the other end, embody the highest fidelity necessary for learning in the market. This deliberate matching of fidelity to purpose ensures resources are used wisely.

Finally, effective prototyping nurtures a culture of iteration and reflection. Prototypes are not endpoints but conversation starters—ways to spark dialogue among designers, users, and stakeholders. When teams internalize prototyping as a continuous rhythm rather than a discrete stage, they shift from asking "is this the right solution?" to exploring "what might we learn next?" In this way, prototyping becomes both a practical strategy and an organizational mindset—anchoring design in curiosity, humility, and the courage to learn by doing (Schrage, 1999).

These strategic mindsets remind us that prototyping is not only about producing artifacts but also about cultivating designers' ability to navigate ambiguity, test ideas responsibly, and evolve solutions collaboratively. Prototyping functions as a deliberate strategy for developing human-centered design competence, strengthening the designer's reflective and empathetic capacity as much as the solution itself (Lauff et al., 2020).

Prototyping as a Way of Thinking

Prototyping, in all its forms, is far more than a technical step in the design process—it is a mindset, a philosophy of inquiry through action. Whether it takes the shape of a napkin sketch, a cardboard model, a digital wireframe, a role-played service, or a fully functioning testbed, the act of prototyping embodies the conviction that design advances by making, testing, and learning. At its heart, prototyping privileges learning over certainty, action over speculation, and iteration over perfection. It is this ethos, more than the artifacts themselves, that makes prototyping central to innovation.

Seen along the continuum of pretotypes, prototypes, and MVPs, this mindset becomes even clearer. Pretotypes challenge whether an idea deserves to exist at all, asking the boldest and cheapest questions. Prototypes move ideas from concept toward tangible form, probing feasibility and user experience. MVPs step into the marketplace, validating viability with real users under real conditions. Together, these approaches form a ladder of experimentation—progressively reducing uncertainty, amplifying learning, and grounding innovation in reality rather than assumption.

Ultimately, prototyping is not confined to a single stage of the design process but becomes the rhythm of design itself: a continuous dialogue between ideas, artifacts, and stakeholders. It sustains innovation by encouraging bold action, reframing failure as learning, and embedding humility in the creative process. In an era of rapid technological change and systemic challenges, this culture of experimentation is not optional but essential. Prototyping reminds us that design is never finished—it is an evolving conversation between possibility and practice, where each iteration teaches us what only making can reveal.

References

Camburn, B., Viswanathan, V., Linsey, J., Anderson, D., Jensen, D., Crawford, R., Otto, K., & Wood, K. (2017). Design prototyping methods: State of the art in strategies, techniques, and guidelines. *Design Science, 3*, e13.

Gibson, I., Rosen, D. W., Stucker, B., & Khorasani, M. (2021). *Additive manufacturing technologies*. Springer.

Houde, S., & Hill, C. (1997). What do prototypes prototype? In M. Helander, T. K. Landauer, & P. Prabhu (Eds.), *Handbook of human-computer interaction* (2nd ed., pp. 367–381). Elsevier.

Lauff, C. A., Knight, D., Kotys-Schwartz, D., & Rentschler, M. E. (2020). The role of prototypes in communication between stakeholders. *Design Studies, 66*, 1–34.

Lim, Y.-K., Stolterman, E., & Tenenberg, J. (2008). The anatomy of prototypes: Prototypes as filters, prototypes as manifestations of design ideas. *ACM Transactions on Computer-Human Interaction, 15*(2), 1–27.

Otto, K. N., & Wood, K. L. (2001). *Product design: Techniques in reverse engineering and new product development*. Prentice Hall.

Ries, E. (2011). *The lean startup: How today's entrepreneurs use continuous innovation to create radically successful businesses*. Crown Business.

Savoia, A. (2019). *Pretotype it: Make sure you are building the right it before you build it right* (2nd ed.). DevMetrix.

Schrage, M. (1999). *Serious play: How the world's best companies simulate to innovate*. Harvard Business School Press.

Ulrich, K. T., & Eppinger, S. D. (2015). *Product design and development* (6th ed.). McGraw-Hill.

Yang, M. C. (2005). A study of prototypes, design activity, and design outcome. *Design Studies, 26*(6), 649–669.

Chapter 9
Design Flexibility

Abstract Change is the norm; flexibility must be designed, not left to chance. We present architectural strategies—modularity, loose coupling, platforming, and real-options thinking—and quantitative methods for valuing flexibility under uncertainty. Readers learn how to design evolvable interfaces and use staged commitments to keep future moves open. The chapter links flexibility to lifecycle costs, resilience, and faster adaptation in products, organizations, and policies.

What Is Design Flexibility

Design flexibility refers to the ease with which a product, system, or process can be adapted or extended to suit evolving conditions, diverse contexts, or unforeseen requirements. Unlike rigid solutions that lock users into fixed forms or functions, flexible designs anticipate change and build adaptability into the very architecture of the system. They are less like static blueprints and more like living frameworks—capable of adjustment and growth over time (Baldwin & Clark, 2000).

Examples of flexible design appear in both the physical and digital worlds. A modular furniture system that can be rearranged to fit different spaces demonstrates physical adaptability, while customizable software that can be reconfigured for new tasks exemplifies digital flexibility. In both cases, the underlying principle is the same: flexibility reduces the friction, cost, and delay of responding to new demands. It transforms design into an open system, prepared not just for current needs but for future possibilities (Ulrich & Eppinger, 2015).

Why Flexibility? Navigating Uncertainty

Flexibility matters because the future is never fixed. The design process unfolds in conditions of uncertainty, where diverse user needs shift, technologies advance, competitors emerge, and social or regulatory pressures evolve. In such contexts,

J. Luo, *Design Science*, Applied Innovation and Technology Management,
https://doi.org/10.1007/978-3-032-13353-3_9

rigid designs quickly become obsolete, while flexible ones remain relevant and resilient. Flexibility delivers more than efficiency. It provides resilience and opportunity. It enables designers to pivot when assumptions prove wrong, scale when opportunities arise, and sustain value over time despite complexity and change.

By lowering the cost of change, flexible designs foster a culture of exploration and continuous learning. They reduce the risks of premature lock-in to suboptimal solutions and keep innovation pathways open. This mirrors the role of pretotyping, prototyping, and MVPs in the design process—rapid trial, feedback, and adjustment—but extends that ethos into the artifact itself. Flexible products and systems can evolve alongside the environments in which they operate, ensuring relevance long after their initial launch.

Tesla's software-updatable vehicles vividly illustrate this principle. Rather than hardwiring all features at the time of manufacturing, Tesla builds flexibility into the car's architecture, enabling over-the-air updates that can improve efficiency, enhance autopilot functions, or add entirely new capabilities. What once required costly redesigns or recalls is now delivered as part of a living, evolving system. This example highlights how embedded flexibility not only sustains value creation but also strengthens long-term competitiveness (Somaya et al., 2020).

Crucially, flexibility is not achieved by accident—it arises from deliberate strategies embedded in product and system architectures, such as real options and platform–family strategies. Real options thinking preserves future choices, much like financial options provide hedges against uncertainty, while platform–family strategies supply the structural foundation that makes such choices technically and economically viable. Together, these approaches transform flexibility from an abstract ideal into a practical design capability. The next sections examine how these strategies interact to operationalize flexibility in practice.

Real Options in Design

The concept of *real options* comes from financial economics, where an option is the right—but not the obligation—to take a certain action in the future, such as buying or selling a stock at a set price. Richard de Neufville and Stefan Scholtes (2011) extended this idea to engineering and design, coining real options to describe design choices that preserve flexibility in the face of uncertainty. In this sense, a real option is a built-in capability within a system, product, or strategy that allows designers and organizations to adapt later—capturing upside opportunities while limiting downside risks.

In design practice, real options manifest in multiple forms. Developing parallel product concepts (e.g., Apple's release of several iPhone variants at different price points and features) keeps strategic pathways open to serve different markets and diverse needs. Designing product families (e.g., Canon's range of printers based on shared core components) creates options for scaling and diversifying without reinventing the wheel. Creating modular subsystems (e.g., Lego bricks or aircraft engine modules) gives designers options to recombine, upgrade, or replace parts as needs change. Each of these examples illustrates how embedding options into design increases resilience and agility. Importantly, the value of these options grows in uncertain contexts—volatile markets, rapidly changing technologies, or unpredictable regulatory environments—because the ability to pivot or scale becomes critical.

Of course, options are not free. Designing for optionality requires upfront investment—whether in parallel development, additional components, or architectural complexity. The challenge lies in structuring options so their benefits outweigh their costs. Too few options, and the system risks rigidity; too many, and the design becomes bloated and uneconomical. Effective real-options thinking therefore requires careful analysis of trade-offs: Which uncertainties matter most? Where does optionality create the greatest leverage? How can costs be contained through modularity, reuse, or scalable architectures?

Ultimately, real options thinking reframes flexibility not as an afterthought but as a deliberate design strategy. By embedding choice into the architecture of products and systems, designers prepare for futures they cannot predict—ensuring that when uncertainty arrives, it is not a threat but an opportunity.

Platform–Family Strategy

One of the most powerful strategies for embedding flexibility into design is the use of platform-based product families. A platform is a stable core—a shared architecture, technology base, or set of components—from which a diverse set of product variants can be developed. In many cases, platforms also span services; treating offerings as product–service systems (PSS) lets firms combine a stable product core with reusable service modules (installation, monitoring, financing, upgrades) to scale variety without fragmenting the system. This approach provides efficiency through reuse while enabling adaptability through variation. Platforms allow organizations to scale innovation by balancing coherence with diversity (Ulrich, 1995; Simpson et al., 2014).

The automotive industry illustrates this principle vividly. Toyota's New Global Architecture (TNGA) provides a common shared chassis and powertrain architecture that underpins multiple vehicle types, from compact sedans to SUVs. By investing once in a robust platform, Toyota reduces design and production costs while retaining the agility to introduce new models quickly. Improvements in safety, efficiency, or electronics made at the platform level cascade across the family, amplifying their impact. Similarly, Apple builds its iPhones on a shared hardware–software ecosystem, allowing multiple models to be released each year while preserving consistency in performance, integration, and brand identity. In both cases, the platform creates a foundation for variety without fragmenting the system.

Flexibility does not come only from swappable parts; it also comes from reusable knowledge—design rules, parametric templates, validated simulation models, test protocols, manufacturing "recipes," and code libraries that travel across variants. When such representations are encoded, searchable, and modular (e.g., pattern catalogs, reference architectures, CAD templates with parameters), teams generate alternatives faster, absorb requirement changes with less rework, and localize risk. In practice, investing in these knowledge artifacts often shortens changeover time more than adding yet another physical option.

At a deeper level, platforms provide coherence: a unifying logic that ensures variants within a family are not just a collection of disconnected offerings but part of an integrated system. Coherence preserves design synergies, strengthens brand consistency, and fosters customer familiarity. Without coherence, variety risks devolving into chaos; with it, platforms achieve the "sweet spot" of flexibility—offering choice to users, efficiency to producers, and resilience to the system as a whole.

Figure 9.1 illustrates an abstract product platform and family. Imagine a system composed of nine basic components, each with a different degree of uncertainty regarding future redesign. Components 1, 2, and 3 are highly stable and thus form the platform, shared across all product variants. The more uncertain components, by contrast, are treated as sources of variety. For example, by creating two, two, three, three, four, and four design options for components 4 through 9, designers can generate a family of 576 potential variants, all built upon the same platform (components 1–3). These variants embody *real options*: even a modest number of alternatives across a few uncertain components can yield an expansive product family, creating massive system-level optionality. This demonstrates how platforms absorb stability while families express flexibility, enabling firms to balance efficiency with adaptability at scale.

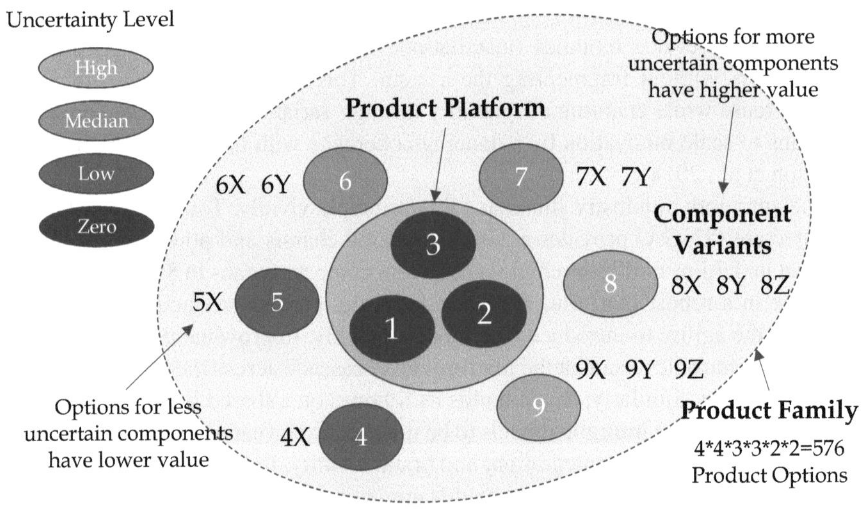

Fig. 9.1 Abstract illustration of a product platform and family

Flexibility in platforms also depends on the degree of openness. Open platforms invite external developers and partners to contribute, extending the ecosystem and generating network effects. IBM's decision to open the architecture of the x86 PC is a classic case: it catalyzed an entire industry of compatible hardware and software, dramatically accelerating adoption, innovation, and ecosystem growth. In contrast, closed platforms retain tighter control, prioritizing integration, quality, and security, as seen in Apple's iOS ecosystem. Closed systems limit external contributions but allow companies to capture more value and maintain strong design integrity. The choice between open and closed platforms is thus a strategic one that shapes not only how flexibility manifests but also how value is created and captured across the ecosystem (Baldwin & Clark, 2000).

In this way, platform and family design, supported by careful decisions about openness and coherence, serve as the structural enablers of real options. They reduce the cost of optionality by leveraging commonalities, extend innovation through ecosystems, and sustain flexibility across time and markets. However, important design questions remain: What belongs in the platform? How should interfaces between variant components and the platform be structured? And to what extent should future uncertainty be deliberately built in the architecture? These questions set the stage for real options thinking as a guiding lens for strategic choices in design.

Principles of Flexible Design

Design flexibility is the capability of a system to be re-designed quickly and inexpensively to meet new or unforeseen requirements. Whether a product or system can evolve depends heavily on its architecture—how components are connected, how interfaces are specified, and how forms are structured. Research on flexible product design highlights four foundational principles—modularity, interface decoupling, parts reduction, and spatial design (Ulrich, 1995; Sanchez & Mahoney, 1996; Tilstra et al., 2015). Together, these principles provide designers with actionable strategies for embedding adaptability directly into artifacts.

Modularity

Modularity lies at the heart of flexible design. By grouping related functions into self-contained modules, designers can isolate changes to specific areas without disrupting the entire system. This allows upgrades, replacements, or expansions to occur quickly and cheaply. To increase modularity, designers may follow several actionable guidelines:

- Use separate modules to carry out unrelated functions.
- Confine functions to single modules.
- Divide larger modules into smaller, interchangeable ones.
- Cluster stable, unlikely-to-change functions into their own modules.

Lego bricks embody modularity perfectly: each brick is a self-contained unit with standardized connectors, enabling endless recombination. In consumer electronics, Fairphone applies modularity by letting users independently replace cameras, batteries, or screens, extending product life and reducing waste. Functional flow models may guide module cuts: map flows, cluster functions, and derive cohesive modules (Stone et al., 2000).

Interface Decoupling

Interfaces—where modules connect and interact—determine whether a system remains rigid or adaptable. Poorly designed interfaces create lock-in, while well-designed ones enable fluid substitution and extension. Decoupling ensures that innovations in one module (e.g., a faster processor) do not cascade into unnecessary redesigns of others. To decouple interfaces, designers can:

- Standardize connectors
- Minimize contact points between modules
- Simplify the geometry of interfaces and components
- Create detachable modules mounted on flexible frameworks
- Use compliant materials or bypass routing for flows of information, energy, or material

The USB standard illustrates effective interface decoupling. By providing a uniform connector, it allows countless devices—keyboards, storage drives, cameras—to connect without redesigning the host system. In aerospace, standardized docking mechanisms on the International Space Station allow modules from different countries to be connected and replaced over time, providing long-term adaptability.

Parts Reduction

The fewer the parts, the fewer the dependencies that constrain adaptation. Reducing part count minimizes dependencies, simplifies manufacturing, and removes constraints on future changes. It also lowers costs and improves reliability. Strategies include:

- Using duplicate or shared parts wherever feasible
- Eliminate unnecessary components
- Sharing functions within modules
- Combining closely related functions within single modules

This principle is common in lean manufacturing and automotive design, where shared parts across product lines reduce cost while enhancing upgrade flexibility.

For example, Dyson vacuum cleaners reduce part count by using cyclonic separation instead of disposable bags and filters, and Toyota practices "parts commonality" in its lean product development, reusing components across multiple models to cut costs while increasing design flexibility. In additive manufacturing (AM), it appears as part consolidation—merging multiple components into a single printable geometry—now a core design-for-AM tactic (Rosen, 2024).

Spatial Design

Flexibility is also shaped by spatial considerations—the physical room left for future modifications. Designs that leave no space for change or expansion become obsolete more quickly. Guidelines include:

- Creating space around modules likely to be changed or expanded
- Providing unobstructed surfaces for new interfaces
- Reserving area along transmission components for potential scaling
- Placing frequently updated parts near the exterior

Data centers embody this principle by leaving server rack space for additional processors or storage, ensuring systems scale with demand. Automotive engine compartments are often designed with extra space for different powertrain options, allowing the same chassis to accommodate gasoline, hybrid, or electric variants.

In sum, these four principles—modularity, decoupling, parts reduction, and spatial design—translate flexibility from a vague aspiration into a set of practical design heuristics. They reduce the cost of change, extend product lifespans, and enable systems to adapt as needs evolve. Flexible design does not happen by accident; it is cultivated through deliberate architectural choices, that anticipate uncertainty and embed resilience into the very fabric of artifacts (Fig. 9.2).

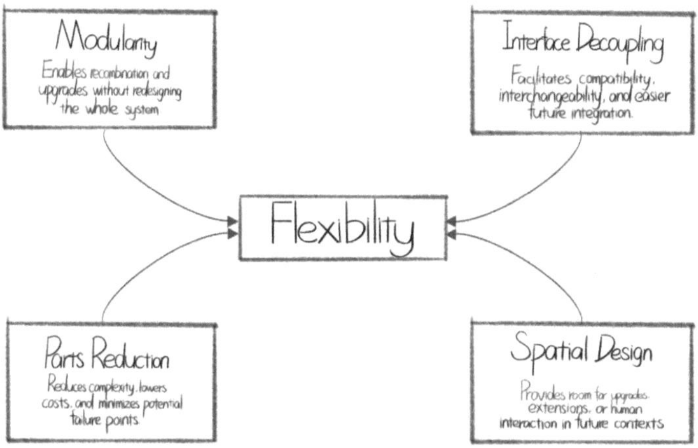

Fig. 9.2 Design-for-Flexibility Principles

Flexibility as Strategic Capacity

Design flexibility transforms uncertainty from a threat into an opportunity. At the operational level, it enables rapid and inexpensive redesigns, turning unexpected changes into learning moments rather than costly setbacks. By embedding flexibility into architecture and interfaces from the outset, designers ensure that systems can evolve without prohibitive cost or delay. Principles such as modularity, interface decoupling, parts reduction, and spatial foresight provide the technical foundation for this adaptability.

Flexibility also operates at a higher strategic level through platform and family strategies. Shared cores, standardized interfaces, and coherent product architectures allow firms to create diverse variants from common foundations. This reduces development costs, accelerates time-to-market, and sustains innovation across markets and generations of products. By carefully balancing openness and coherence, platforms extend their impact outward, creating ecosystems of complementary offerings that multiply value and resilience.

Ultimately, platforms and flexible design principles combine to generate real options in design—preserving future choices, hedging against uncertainty, and creating pathways to capture upside opportunities while limiting downside risks. In this way, flexibility becomes more than a design attribute; it is a strategic capacity. Far from being an afterthought, it is an enabler of sustainable innovation in an era defined by rapid technological change, shifting markets, and complex societal challenges. Flexible design ensures not only responsiveness to change, but also the capability of shaping it.

References

Baldwin, C. Y., & Clark, K. B. (2000). *Design rules: The power of modularity*. MIT Press.
de Neufville, R., & Scholtes, S. (2011). *Flexibility in engineering design*. MIT Press.
Rosen, D. W. (2024). The current Design for Additive Manufacturing frontier. *International Journal of Precision Engineering and Manufacturing-Smart Technology, 2*, 1–14.
Sanchez, R., & Mahoney, J. T. (1996). Modularity, flexibility, and knowledge management in product and organization design. *Strategic Management Journal, 17*(S2), 63–76.
Simpson, T. W., Jiao, J., Siddique, Z., & Hölttä-Otto, K. (Eds.). (2014). *Advances in product family and product platform design: Methods & applications*. Springer.
Somaya, D., Puranam, P., & Wilcox King, Z. (2020). *Tesla: Software updates and flexibility in automotive design*. Harvard Business School Case Collection.
Stone, R. B., Wood, K. L., & Crawford, R. H. (2000). A heuristic method to identify modules from a functional description of a product. *Journal of Mechanical Design, 122*(4), 359–370.
Tilstra, A. H., Backlund, P. B., Seepersad, C. C., & Wood, K. L. (2015). Principles for designing products with flexibility for future evolution. *International Journal of Mass Customization, 5*(1), 22–54.
Ulrich, K. (1995). The role of product architecture in the manufacturing firm. *Research Policy, 24*(3), 419–440.
Ulrich, K. T., & Eppinger, S. D. (2015). *Product design and development* (6th ed.). McGraw-Hill Education.

Chapter 10
Design Convergence

Abstract Convergence is disciplined choice under constraints. This chapter structures multi-objective decision-making, verification/validation, and traceability from assumptions to evidence. We cover local vs. global optima, rugged performance landscapes, strategies for escaping traps, and selecting among alternatives via clear criteria. Heuristics are combined with optimization to stage tests that de-risk commitments. Throughout, we emphasize auditability—decisions that "hold in the world" because they are justified, reproducible, and aligned with requirements, values, and limits.

Divergence and Convergence in Design

Design is not a straight line from problem to solution but an iterative rhythm of divergence and convergence. Divergence expands the design space—exploring possibilities through broad ideation, reframing of problems, and alternative pathways. Convergence, by contrast, narrows the design space—evaluating, filtering, and selecting among alternatives to identify the most promising options. Divergence generates variety, while convergence distills clarity. Together, these dual movements form the heartbeat of the design process—a cycle of expansion and contraction that keeps ideas alive while moving them toward realization.

Psychologists as early as Guilford (1950) distinguished between divergent thinking, which generates multiple possibilities, and convergent thinking, which drives toward single, best answers. Design leverages both modes: divergence fuels creativity and novelty, while convergence imposes discipline and selectivity. Effective designers learn to oscillate between these modes fluidly, balancing imagination with judgment.

This rhythm is reflected in classic models of innovation. The Double Diamond Model distinguishes between discover and develop as divergent phases, and define and deploy as convergent ones. Similarly, the Double-Hump Innovation Model frames opportunity discovery and design generation as divergence, and opportunity evaluation and design evaluation as convergence. Across these frameworks, the

J. Luo, *Design Science*, Applied Innovation and Technology Management,
https://doi.org/10.1007/978-3-032-13353-3_10

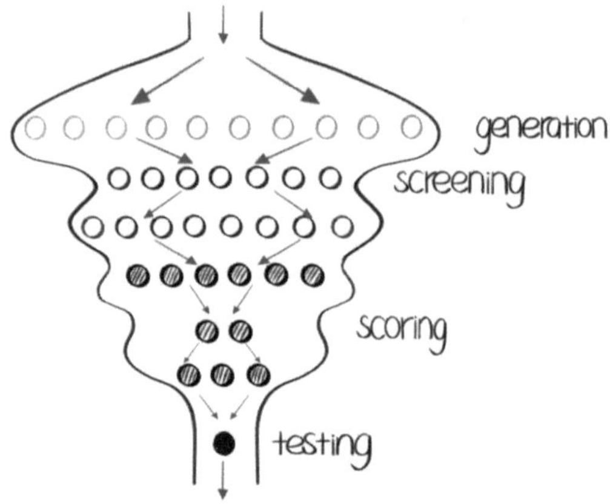

Fig. 10.1 The concept development funnel (Wheelwright & Clark, 1992)

message is consistent: innovation requires the integration of creative divergence and disciplined convergence—the capacity to explore widely and focus sharply.

The Concept Development Funnel illustrates how convergence unfolds in practice (Wheelwright & Clark, 1992). Designers typically begin with a large pool of raw ideas, progressively narrowed through concept generation, screening (eliminating weak options), scoring (comparing alternatives with criteria), and testing (prototyping or user validation). Crucially, the funnel is not purely linear. Promising fragments of pre-screened ideas may be recombined, temporarily enlarging the option set, while iteration across stages sharpens outcomes. Convergence here is iterative as well as selective—better concepts emerge through cycles of filtering, recombination, and refinement. The funnel thus frames convergence as a disciplined yet flexible process that channels creativity, reduces uncertainty, and moves toward robust design decisions (Fig. 10.1).

Importantly, convergence is not just about efficiency; it is also about learning. A "final" concept rarely appears in the first pass. Instead, convergence often stimulates fresh insights: weaknesses revealed in evaluation inspire improvements or hybrids, while comparison across alternatives highlights trade-offs and hidden opportunities. In this sense, convergence is not the end of creativity but its transformation—from generating sheer quantity to sharpening quality. Ultimately, through successive cycles of screening, scoring, and testing, designers converge on concepts robust enough to justify deeper investment in prototyping, optimization, and development.

Design Evaluation and Selection

If divergence is about opening possibilities, convergence is about making choices. Once designers have generated a wide array of concepts, they face the critical task of deciding which ones to pursue. This stage of evaluation and selection is where creativity meets judgment, and where ideas begin their transition from possibility to probability. Effective evaluation is neither a single decision nor a final judgment—it is a series of cycles through which ideas are compared, refined, and recombined until a smaller set of high-potential concepts emerges.

Decision Heuristics

At the most intuitive level, designers often rely on heuristics—fast, experience-based rules that allow efficient decisions under uncertainty. Decision science has shown that such heuristics can be surprisingly effective, especially in the early stages when information is incomplete and time is limited. The recognition heuristic encourages decision-makers to favor the familiar; the take-the-best heuristic selects the option with the most discriminating positive attribute; elimination by aspects rules out candidates that fail to meet minimum thresholds; and category elimination quickly narrows the field by removing entire groups of less promising alternatives. These heuristics are not flawless, but they provide efficient ways of cutting through complexity when rapid progress is required (Gigerenzer & Goldstein, 1996).

Group Techniques

When decisions involve multiple stakeholders or expertise, designers often turn to structured group techniques. Methods like the Q-sort allow experts to collaboratively rank concepts by sorting them into ordered categories, building consensus through discussion rather than dictation (Stephenson, 1953). Similarly, the Delphi method can be used to aggregate expert judgment iteratively, helping groups move toward convergence even in the face of uncertainty (Linstone & Turoff, 1975). These approaches are particularly valuable when no single individual possesses complete knowledge of all design dimensions, and when legitimacy depends on collective buy-in.

Systematic Frameworks

Beyond heuristics and group consensus, designers often employ systematic evaluation frameworks that provide more traceability and rigor. A widely adopted example is the two-stage process of screening and scoring (Ulrich et al., 2020). The first stage, concept screening, provides a quick, approximate comparison that eliminates clearly inferior options. The second stage, concept scoring, applies weighted criteria in a more detailed and quantitative fashion, allowing finer distinctions among surviving concepts. Screening provides efficiency by narrowing the field, while scoring ensures rigor in selecting among the finalists. This staged approach balances efficiency with thoroughness, ensuring that promising ideas are not prematurely discarded while keeping decision-making manageable.

One of the most influential and nuanced frameworks in this category is the Pugh Method, or Concept Selection Matrix. Often mischaracterized as a simple scoring tool, Pugh himself emphasized it as "controlled convergence" (Pugh, 1981): an iterative process where evaluation is not a terminal filter but a generator of new insights and hybrids.

The method begins by selecting a datum—a baseline concept that is well understood and reasonably strong. Alternative designs are then compared against this baseline in a matrix, with judgments recorded as better (+), worse (−), or same (0). Table 10.1 presents a simple illustrative Pugh chart. In this case, Concept 1 can be screened out immediately, as it is dominated by Concept 2 across all criteria.

What makes the Pugh Method powerful is not the tabulation itself, but the structured discussion it provokes. Teams systematically "attack the negatives," identifying weaknesses and often creating hybrids that combine strengths across alternatives. For example, in the illustrative table, Concept 2 performs strongly overall but is weak on Criterion 4; by borrowing features from Concept 3, which excels in that area, the team can generate a hybrid concept stronger across all five criteria. In this way, negative assessments become springboards for improvement, and evaluation evolves into a creative act rather than a purely eliminative one.

Importantly, Pugh stressed that multiple runs of the matrix are expected. The first pass may only eliminate dominated options, while subsequent runs refine survivors, incorporate new knowledge, and converge toward stronger concepts. As Frey et al. (2009) highlighted, the Pugh process simulates a design team engaged in cycles of evaluation, ideation, and investigation. Compared to formal decision-analytic methods that collapse criteria into a single utility score, the Pugh Method remains coarse-grained and heuristic, avoiding the false precision of numerical ratings that can foster misplaced confidence in rough estimates. Instead, it emphasizes relative judgments and fact-based discussion, encouraging objectivity while reducing emotional attachment to favored concepts.

Finally, the Pugh Method is not merely about trade-offs. While many traditional decision frameworks emphasize compromise (e.g., pay more for higher quality, sacrifice weight for durability), Pugh advocated on creative convergence that seeks

Table 10.1 An illustrative Pugh table

	Datum	Concept 1	Concept 2	Concept 3
Criterion 1	0	+	+	−
Criterion 2	0	−	+	0
Criterion 3	0	+	+	+
Criterion 4	0	−	−	+
Criterion 5	0	−	+	+
Sum +		2	4	3
Sum −		3	1	1
Sum 0		0	0	1

Table 10.2 The Pugh Method for controlled convergence

Element	Essence
Purpose	A systematic yet creative framework for concept evaluation and selection. Goes beyond scoring to stimulate *controlled convergence*
Core principles	Controlled convergence: iterative, generative cycles Relative judgment: compare concepts to a baseline (+, −, *0*) Creativity through evaluation: weaknesses inspire hybrids Objectivity with flexibility: fact-based, avoids premature lock-in
Steps	1. Select a datum (baseline concept) 2. Construct the matrix (alternatives × criteria) 3. Compare each alternative to the datum (+, −, *0*) 4. Analyze results to identify strong and weak concepts 5. Attack negatives to generate improvements or hybrids 6. Iterate with multiple runs, refining survivors
Outcomes	Eliminate weak options Strengthen promising ones Stimulate hybrids and new concepts Build consensus and objectivity
Key idea	Not just choosing among trade-offs, but advancing beyond trade-offs through iteration and recombination

advances beyond trade-offs—designs that leapfrog existing options. By encouraging recombination and iteration, controlled convergence helps generate concepts capable of out-competing dominant designs and reshaping the state of the art (Table 10.2).

Evaluation does not mark the end of the design journey. Surviving concepts move forward into detailed design, prototyping, and testing, where their assumptions are exposed to real-world scrutiny. In fact, evaluation and prototyping are tightly coupled: early-stage evaluations guide what gets prototyped, while prototype feedback informs subsequent rounds of selection. In this way, convergence is not a single narrowing pass but an iterative, learning-oriented cycle.

Together, heuristics, group techniques, and systematic methods form a toolkit for design convergence. Each has its place: heuristics provide speed, group methods provide legitimacy, and structured matrices provide rigor. The art of convergence lies in knowing when to apply each, and how to cycle among them as ideas mature. Used thoughtfully, these approaches ensure that convergence is not an arbitrary elimination of options but a disciplined transformation of ideas into viable, testable candidates for optimization and development.

Design Optimization

Once a design team has converged on a promising concept or a confined design space, the next challenge is optimization: systematically searching for the best detailed design within the defined space of functions, parameters, and constraints. If evaluation and selection narrow a broad pool of concepts to a manageable set of viable candidates, optimization sharpens these candidates further—driving toward specific solutions that maximize performance, minimize cost, or balance multiple objectives.

At its core, optimization translates design convergence into a quantitative process. Designers define objective functions (e.g., minimize weight, maximize efficiency, optimize user comfort), specify constraints (e.g., safety regulations, manufacturability limits, budget thresholds), and then search for parameter values that achieve the best trade-offs. In this sense, optimization formalizes the enduring challenge of "making the best design possible" under competing demands.

Importantly, modeling the design space mathematically does more than narrow choices—it also opens new possibilities. By formalizing objectives, constraints, and relationships, designers can explore a relatively more "continuous" parameter space rather than being confined to a few discrete concepts. Optimization thus expands the landscape of feasible options even as it guides the search toward the best ones, creating a disciplined interplay between exploration and convergence. Structured in this way, more alternatives can be generated, tested, and refined, ultimately leading to deeper insights and more robust solutions.

A general design optimization problem can then be expressed in a standard mathematical form (multiple objectives subject to equality and inequality constraints) as follows:

$$\begin{array}{ll} \textit{Minimize / Maximize} & f_1(x), f_2(x), \ldots, f_k(x) \\ \text{Subject to} & g_j(x) \le 0, \quad j = 1, \ldots, m \\ & h_l(x) = 0, \quad l = 1, \ldots, p \\ \text{Where} & x = (x_1, x_2, \ldots, x_n) \in R^n \end{array}$$

Here, x represents the design decision variables (e.g., dimensions, material choices, control settings); $f_i(x)$ for $i = 1, \ldots, k$ are the objective functions to be optimized (e.g., minimizing weight, minimizing cost, maximizing efficiency, maximizing comfort); and the g_j and h_l terms represent constraints, which may be inequalities (e.g., safety and functionality limits, manufacturability requirements) or equalities (e.g., equilibrium conditions), respectively. This general formulation highlights the essence of optimization in design: navigating a high-dimensional space of possible solutions to satisfy multiple objectives while respecting real-world constraints.

To solve such a multi-objective design problem (e.g., trading off weight, stiffness, and cost), three complementary approaches are common. Pareto search generates a set of non-dominated designs so trade-offs are visible and selection remains value-driven. Scalarization collapses multiple goals into a single weighted score—simple and solver-friendly, especially when the frontier is well behaved. The epsilon-constraint method optimizes one focal objective while treating the others as explicit limits, sweeping those limits to map trade-offs and handle non-convex fronts.

In practice, designers normalize objectives, start with a global exploratory search to reveal the landscape, then locally refine a few promising designs. Teams use clear visuals (e.g., Pareto plots, parallel coordinates) to communicate trade-offs, and run sensitivity checks on weights or limits to test robustness. The team keeps feasibility central (stress, deflection, manufacturability). The outcome is not a single "answer," but a transparent Pareto set from which the team can deliberately converge on a solution aligned with goals, costs, and constraints.

Local Versus Global Optimization

A central issue in optimization is distinguishing between local and global optima (Fig. 10.2). Local search methods, such as gradient descent or hill-climbing, adjust parameters incrementally to improve performance. They are efficient and precise, well-suited for exploitation of a promising region of the design space, but they risk becoming trapped in suboptimal solutions. To escape these traps, designers often turn to global search techniques that deliberately broaden the search. Examples include evolutionary algorithms, which simulate biological processes of mutation and selection (Holland, 1975); genetic algorithms, which evolve populations of candidate solutions through recombination (Goldberg, 1989); and simulated annealing, which accepts occasional "worse" solutions to avoid premature convergence (Kirkpatrick et al., 1983). These approaches prioritize exploration, probing across the design landscape to uncover alternative peaks and more radical possibilities.

In this sense, the distinction between local and global optimization echoes James March's seminal insight on the tension between exploitation and exploration. Exploitation ensures efficiency, reliability, and refinement of known solutions,

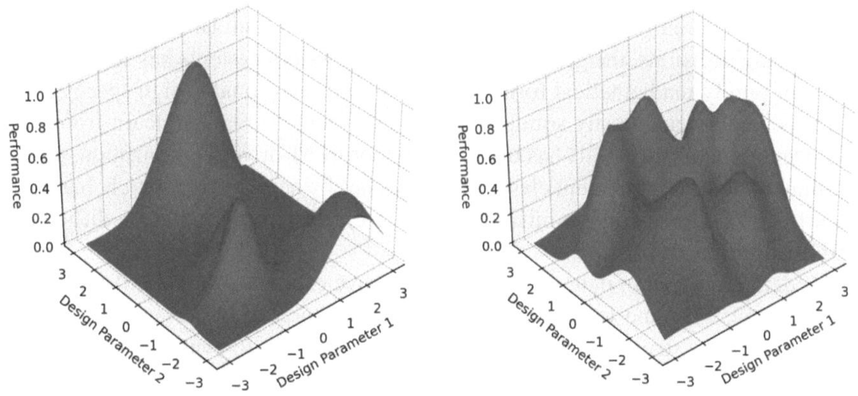

Fig. 10.2 Rugged performance landscapes: two illustrative performance surfaces (3 and 8 peaks, respectively) in a 2D design space (2 parameters on the axes). As ruggedness increases, local optima proliferate and the global optimum becomes harder to find, highlighting the need for global search and disciplined convergence

while exploration sustains novelty, adaptability, and resilience in the face of uncertainty (March, 1991). Successful design optimization requires balancing these dual imperatives—too much exploitation risks premature lock-in to local optima, while too much exploration risks aimless search without actionable convergence. In practice, the most effective optimization strategies combine exploitation and exploration dynamically: using global methods to identify promising regions of the design space, and local methods to refine them with precision. This interplay not only improves solution quality but also mirrors how organizations, teams, and natural systems innovate—through cycles of focused refinement and expansive discovery.

The integration of exploration and exploitation has been a central theme in optimization-based design, pioneered by Panos Papalambros and Douglass Wilde (2000). Their work formalized how mathematical programming and computational optimization can be applied to multi-objective, multidisciplinary systems, integrating analysis tools, constraint management, and decision criteria into systematic frameworks. They showed how objectives, constraints, and models can be combined to support both rigorous analysis and iterative refinement.

Crucially, this approach positioned optimization not merely as a numerical technique but as a design philosophy—a structured way of organizing the search for solutions that is disciplined yet adaptive, precise yet open to discovery. In this sense, optimization-based design offers a systematic means of balancing March's (1991) tension between exploitation and exploration: enabling efficient refinement of known solutions while leaving room for broader discovery and creative divergence. By embedding optimization into the design process itself, convergence on solutions does not come at the expense of generating new possibilities.

AI-Driven Optimization

While optimization-based design established a rigorous foundation for structuring engineering decisions, the growing complexity of modern systems has stretched the limits of purely mathematical formulations. High-dimensional design spaces, nonlinear behaviors, and costly simulations demand methods that can learn from data and adapt dynamically. This has opened the door to AI-driven optimization, where learning systems complement classical approaches by accelerating search, handling uncertainty, and revealing promising regions of the design space that are difficult to find by intuition alone.

Modern advances in data-driven modeling have expanded the toolkit for design optimization. Machine learning–based approaches such as Bayesian optimization enable efficient search in high-dimensional, expensive-to-evaluate spaces—for example, tuning aerodynamic shapes when each simulation run is costly. Surrogate models approximate the response surface so designers can evaluate, screen, and iterate rapidly before committing to high-fidelity analysis. Together, these methods complement classical optimization by blending deterministic rigor with probabilistic exploration: they make trade-offs explicit, reduce evaluation cost, and steer attention toward the most informative experiments (Shahriari et al., 2016; Garnett, 2023; He et al., 2023).

Generative algorithms, especially large language models (LLMs), push this further via an iterative generate-test-learn loop. Beyond drafting designs or code and coordinating simulators, LLMs can encode structural context and domain rules to guide the optimization process, and reported studies show faster convergence to better solutions relative to traditional mathematical optimization techniques. LLMs can also augment Bayesian optimization and evolutionary search by encoding constraints and preferences in natural language, shaping priors or acquisition heuristics, seeding diverse mutations, and repairing infeasible designs. Used this way, LLMs act as tool-orchestrating planners that blend broad exploration with local refinement while respecting constraints. To keep that creativity disciplined, designers may pair AI models with verifiers and simulators, log prompts for reproducibility, and enforce hard constraints via programmatic checks (Austin et al., 2024; Jiang et al., 2024; Liu et al., 2024; Yang et al., 2024).

Examples of Design Optimization

Design optimization principles extend across scales and industries, from advanced engineering systems to everyday products. The examples in Table 10.3 show how local, global, and AI-driven approaches complement one another—balancing exploitation and exploration to achieve robust solutions. In aerospace, automotive, and consumer products alike, optimization serves both refinement and discovery: local methods exploit known solutions with precision, global methods broaden the search for novel alternatives, and AI-driven methods integrate both by intelligently navigating complex, high-dimensional spaces. Together, these approaches make convergence not a simple narrowing act but a dynamic process that yields robust and innovative outcomes.

Despite their power, optimization methods are not a substitute for design judgment. They ultimately depend on the objectives and constraints defined by humans, which, in turn, are shaped by broader goals, values, and contexts. An overly narrow formulation may yield technically "optimal" solutions that fail to address real-world needs. Optimization should therefore be seen not as the end of design, but as a disciplined phase within the larger rhythm of divergence and convergence.

In practice, design optimization remains iterative. Models are built, solutions are tested, constraints are updated, and objectives are refined. Each round sharpens understanding, often revealing new trade-offs or overlooked possibilities. Optimization, then, is less about arriving at a single final answer than about progressively aligning design intent, performance goals, and practical feasibility—a continual process of learning and adjustment that strengthens both the solution and the designer's insight.

Table 10.3 Illustrations of design optimization across domains

Design domain	Aircraft wing	EV battery pack	Ergonomic chair
Design challenge	Refine wing geometry for aerodynamic efficiency and structural strength	Balance energy density, thermal safety, cost, and longevity	Optimize comfort and inclusivity for diverse body types
Local optimization (Exploitation): Provides efficiency and precision but risks premature lock-in to local optima	Incrementally adjust camber, angle of attack, or thickness distribution to improve lift-to-drag ratio	Fine-tune cell spacing or cooling channel dimensions to optimize thermal management	Adjust seat angle, lumbar curvature, or armrest positions incrementally based on user feedback
Global optimization (Exploration): Broadens discovery and avoids local traps by searching across the design landscape	Use genetic algorithms or simulated annealing to explore unconventional geometries across the design landscape	Explore diverse pack layouts and cooling strategies with evolutionary search	Explore broader chair geometries and adjustment ranges using evolutionary algorithms on anthropometric datasets
AI-driven optimization: Accelerates convergence in complex spaces while enabling creative exploration	Surrogate models and Bayesian optimization accelerate CFD-driven wing design in high-dimensional spaces	Machine learning predicts performance and degradation across thousands of candidate designs	AI-based biomechanical and comfort models predict pressure distribution, fatigue, and usability across diverse populations

Design Convergence in Industry: Emergence of Dominant Design

Design convergence does not end at the team or organization level; industries also converge. Over time, markets sift through competing architectures, interfaces, and feature bundles until a dominant design emerges—an accepted “recipe” that defines what a product is and how it should work. This is not a single model so much as a set of design rules and architectural choices that coordinate the actions of producers, suppliers, and users. Framed in the book’s 3A perspective, dominant design reflects Actors aligning around shared Actions (standards, compatibility, manufacturing routines) that stabilize the Artifact architecture and enable scaling.

The Abernathy–Utterback Model of industry dynamics (Fig. 10.3) describe a recognizable arc: an era of ferment (high variety, experimental architectures), a transition as selection pressures intensify (performance, reliability, cost, complement availability), and an era of specific design in which the dominant architecture standardizes interfaces and features (Abernathy & Utterback, 1978). As the architecture stabilizes, innovation shifts from product to process: firms invest in tooling, quality control, supply-chain optimization, and cost reduction. Performance

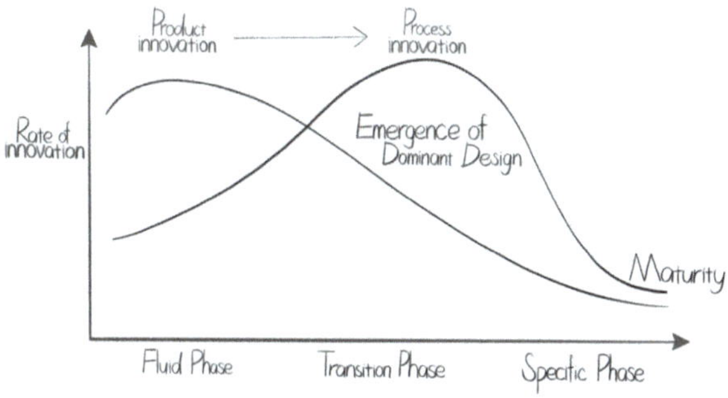

Fig. 10.3 Industry dynamics and emergence of dominant design (Abernathy & Utterback, 1978)

continues to improve, but along the trajectory defined by the dominant design rather than by architectural leaps (Utterback, 1994).

Several mechanisms drive industry-level design convergence.

- Demand-side learning and expectations. Users gravitate to familiar form factors and interaction patterns; training and habits create switching costs.
- Supply-side scale and learning curves. Shared architectures support component reuse, specialized suppliers, and cumulative know-how that lowers cost and raises quality.
- Network effects and complementarity. The value of a design grows with the installed base and the availability of complements (software, accessories, infrastructure); compatibility becomes a strategic asset.
- Standard-setting and governance. Formal consortia and de facto leaders codify interfaces, certification regimes, and reference designs that reduce uncertainty for ecosystem participants.

Dominant design reshapes how organizations innovate. Teams redirect effort from exploring rival architectures to optimizing a settled one—tightening tolerances, improving reliability, and simplifying assembly. Design roadmaps prioritize component-level innovation and modular upgrades; platform owners curate interface stability while adding features at the edges. Market structure consolidates around a smaller set of viable producers, while upstream suppliers specialize and achieve scale. The unit of competition shifts from "which architecture" to "whose implementation is better, cheaper, and more reliable."

Design dominance creates clarity, but it also creates lock-in. Path dependence can entrench suboptimal choices; interface inertia can slow response to new technologies or use cases. Firms that thrive post-convergence cultivate optionality: they design for modular substitution, maintain upgrade paths, and experiment at the periphery without breaking compatibility. Meanwhile, entrants may pursue architectural or disruptive innovation—introducing new performance dimensions or usage models that make the dominant trajectory less relevant.

To capture the benefits of dominance while mitigating lock-in, designers and organizations can adopt the following phase-specific design playbook.

- Era of ferment: run multiple architectural bets, prototype aggressively, seed complements, and learn with lead users.
- Transition to dominance: emphasize interoperability, reduce user adoption friction, and invest in standards work; decide what to open vs. keep proprietary.
- Era of specific design: lock interfaces, shift to process and platform optimization, and extend the ecosystem through modules and services—while scanning for discontinuities that may reset the game.

Taken together, these actions channel creativity into architectures the market can scale, without sacrificing strategic flexibility.

Industry-level design convergence converts plural possibilities into a shared design language that enables scale. For designers, the task is twofold: shape the emergence of dominance when possible (through standards, complements, and clear architectural choices) and exploit it once established (through process excellence and modular evolution)—all while guarding against the complacency that dominance invites. In short, convergence at the industry level disciplines creativity without extinguishing it; it channels invention into architectures that markets can understand, adopt, and grow.

Convergence as Discipline

Convergence is not the end of creativity; it is the discipline that turns possibility into commitment. At the team level, convergence begins with lightweight judgment and gradually layers in structure. Heuristics and facilitated group techniques help people choose when information is scarce; screening and scoring introduce order as evidence accumulates; and Pugh's "controlled convergence" treats evaluation as a creative act—comparing to a datum, attacking negatives, and deliberately generating hybrids. What survives moves into prototyping and test, and the feedback loops back to reshape criteria and concepts. In this mode, convergence is a loop rather than a gate: it privileges traceable reasoning over advocacy and treats numbers as aids to judgment, not substitutes for it.

Optimization adds a quantitative backbone to that loop. By defining objectives, constraints, and models, designers search a relatively more "continuous" space of alternatives and make trade-offs explicit. Crucially, modeling widens as well as narrows: it reveals promising regions that intuition might miss and then guides fine-grained refinement within them. Effective practice balances global search (exploration) and local search (exploitation), echoing March's insight that progress requires both; classical optimization provides rigor, and modern AI methods—surrogates, Bayesian search, and generative algorithms—provide speed and reach. None of these replaces design judgment; they amplify it when the questions are well posed.

Convergence also unfolds at the industry level. As markets learn, architecture stabilizes and a dominant design emerges, coordinating producers, suppliers, and users around shared rules and interfaces; innovation then shifts from architectural bets to process excellence, platform stewardship, and component-level improvement. The clarity that enables scaling can also create lock-in, so disciplined convergence preserves optionality through modular interfaces, healthy complements, and vigilant scanning for discontinuities. Practiced well, convergence delivers fewer but better bets, auditable choices, and architectures that can be manufactured, maintained, and extended—channeling creativity into outcomes that are testable, optimizable, and ultimately scalable.

References

Abernathy, W. J., & Utterback, J. M. (1978). Patterns of industrial innovation. *Technology Review, 80*(7), 40–47.

Austin, D. E., Korikov, A., Toroghi, A., & Sanner, S. (2024). Bayesian optimization with LLM-based acquisition functions for natural language preference elicitation. In *Proceedings of the 18th ACM Conference on Recommender Systems (RecSys '24)*. ACM.

Frey, D. D., Herder, P. M., Wijnia, Y., Subrahmanian, E., Katsikopoulos, K. V., De Neufville, R., & Clausing, D. P. (2009). The Pugh controlled convergence method: Model-based evaluation and implications for design. *Research in Engineering Design, 20*(1), 41–58.

Garnett, R. (2023). *Bayesian optimization*. Cambridge University Press.

Gigerenzer, G., & Goldstein, D. G. (1996). Reasoning the fast and frugal way: Models of bounded rationality. *Psychological Review, 103*(4), 650–669.

Goldberg, D. E. (1989). *Genetic algorithms in search, optimization, and machine learning*. Addison-Wesley.

Guilford, J. P. (1950). Creativity. *American Psychologist, 5*(9), 444–454.

He, C., Zhang, Y., Gong, D., & Ji, X. (2023). A review of surrogate-assisted evolutionary algorithms for expensive optimization problems. *Expert Systems with Applications, 217*, 119495.

Holland, J. H. (1975). *Adaptation in natural and artificial systems*. University of Michigan Press.

Jiang, S., Xie, M., & Luo, J. (2024). Large language models for combinatorial optimization of design structure matrix. In *Proceedings of the 25th International Conference on Engineering Design (ICED '25)*, Dallas, Texas.

Kirkpatrick, S., Gelatt, C. D., Jr., & Vecchi, M. P. (1983). Optimization by simulated annealing. *Science, 220*(4598), 671–680.

Linstone, H. A., & Turoff, M. (1975). *The Delphi method: Techniques and applications*. Addison-Wesley.

Liu, T., Astorga, N., Seedat, N., & van der Schaar, M. (2024). Large language models to enhance Bayesian optimization. In *Proceedings of the International Conference on Learning Representations (ICLR 2024)*, Vienna, Austria.

March, J. G. (1991). Exploration and exploitation in organizational learning. *Organization Science, 2*(1), 71–87.

Papalambros, P. Y., & Wilde, D. J. (2000). *Principles of optimal design: Modeling and computation* (2nd ed.). Cambridge University Press.

Pugh, S. (1981). Concept selection: A method that works. In *Proceedings of the International Conference on Engineering Design (ICED)*, Rome, Italy.

Shahriari, B., Swersky, K., Wang, Z., Adams, R. P., & De Freitas, N. (2016). Taking the human out of the loop: A review of Bayesian optimization. *Proceedings of the IEEE, 104*(1), 148–175.

Stephenson, W. (1953). *The study of behavior: Q-technique and its methodology*. University of Chicago Press.

Ulrich, K. T., Eppinger, S. D., & Yang, M. C. (2020). *Product design and development* (7th ed.). McGraw-Hill Education.

Utterback, J. M. (1994). *Mastering the dynamics of innovation: How companies can seize opportunities in the face of technological change*. Harvard Business School Press.

Wheelwright, S. C., & Clark, K. B. (1992). *Revolutionizing product development: Quantum leaps in speed, efficiency, and quality*. Free Press.

Yang, C., Wang, X., Lu, Y., Liu, H., Le, Q. V., Zhou, D., & Chen, X. (2024). Large language models as optimizers. In *Proceedings of the International Conference on Learning Representations (ICLR 2024)*.

Chapter 11
Design Complexity

Abstract Complexity emerges from dependencies: structure governs behavior. This chapter equips designers to see and steer complexity using tools such as Design Structure Matrices (DSMs) and change-propagation analysis. We show how to expose hidden couplings, localize risk, partition architectures, and design interfaces that contain rework. Case patterns connect system architecture to emergent behaviors and socio-technical coupling, offering tactics to align product, process, and organizational architectures so systems remain evolvable, testable, and governable.

Why Complexity Matters

As designs advance, failure rarely comes from any single part; it comes from interactions multiplying. As components, functions, and stakeholders grow, dependencies introduce feedback, delay, and surprise. Technically, small changes can ripple into rework, performance regressions, or outright incompatibilities. Managerially, coordination costs rise as schedules slip, interfaces drift, and accountability blurs (Eppinger, 2001). In short, complexity is less about how many elements a system contains and more about how many ways those elements depend on one another.

The practical response begins with reductionism: decompose to manage, by level. Work becomes tractable when it is divided into units that fit human cognitive limits and clear ownership lines, from system down to component:

- Product → subsystems → modules → components
- Process → sub-processes → tasks
- Organization → teams → individuals

Decomposition clarifies responsibility, shortens feedback loops, and localizes most problem-solving, but cross-level dependencies persist, so decomposition must be paired with deliberate re-integration (interfaces, contracts, and tests) to deliver performance.

Most designed systems are nearly decomposable—strong interactions within modules, weaker ones across them (Simon, 1962)—and this pattern often holds

J. Luo, *Design Science*, Applied Innovation and Technology Management,
https://doi.org/10.1007/978-3-032-13353-3_11

across levels. Modules can therefore be developed semi-independently; yet residual cross-module ties still shape global behavior. Because performance lives in the interfaces—how parts connect, how information flows, and how decisions traverse boundaries—integration remains essential. Without deliberate integration, local optimizations pull at cross-purposes and small edits become large problems.

Architecture by Design

Architecture is the discipline that makes integration work. It is the designed pattern of interactions that governs behavior over time (Crawley et al., 2004), turning connections into explicit rules and contracts, such as signals, tolerances, protocols, and verification, so outcomes are governed rather than left to chance. Architecture operates across levels—system, subsystem, module, component—assigning responsibilities and interface contracts at higher levels before committing to component detail.

A well-designed architecture concentrates on life-cycle qualities (often called "ilities"), such as reliability that sustains function under stress, flexibility that adapts to new needs, and evolvability that improves across generations. It also manages emergence, i.e., the system-level effects that arise from parts interacting, so the same connectivity that enables load-sharing does not propagate failures or create policy resistance. In practice, good architecture minimizes gratuitous complexity while preserving the essential complexity performance demands, stabilizes and versions interfaces, and places decouplers or redundancy where propagation risk concentrates.

Here, architecture is treated as a triad (Fig. 11.1) to be co-designed: the product's structure of components and interfaces, the process' sequence of activities and feedback loops, and the organization's patterns of communication and decision rights. These architectures are long-lived and co-evolve with standards, legacy, and stakeholder needs. When they align, change propagates predictably, schedules stabilize, and quality scales; when they drift, coordination frays and complexity turns from a design fact into a management hazard. Managing design complexity is therefore not about eliminating it, but about designing and maintaining an architecture that delivers required function while suppressing undesirable emergence.

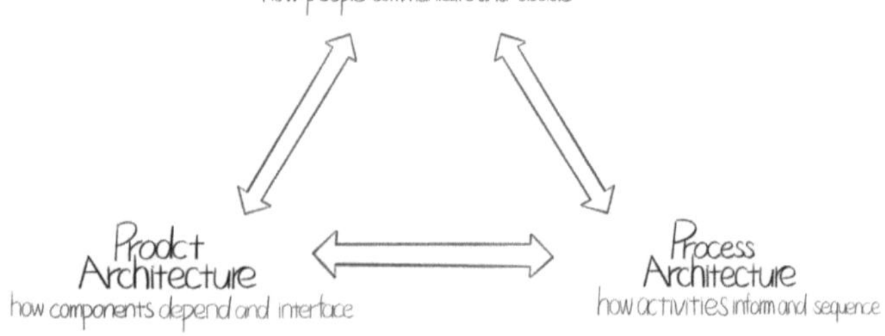

Fig. 11.1 The product-process-organization (PPO) triad architecture

Design Structure Matrix

Complexity becomes tractable when its structure is visible. The Design Structure Matrix (DSM)—also called a Dependency Structure Matrix—is a compact, square map of who depends on whom inside a system. Rows and columns list the same elements (a component, an activity, a parameter, or a team); a mark at position *(i, j)* means "*i* depends on *j*" (Steward, 1981). This spare encoding keeps every interaction on a single page and turns architecture into something we can analyze and redesign (Fig. 11.2).

A DSM works because it matches the grain of real design decisions. When we ask architectural questions—what belongs together and what should be separated—the matrix shows clusters as visible blocks along the diagonal. When we ask process questions—what ordering reduces rework and where iteration will bite—off-diagonal feedbacks and cycles stand out as bands we can break, buffer, or resequence (Eppinger & Browning, 2012). Unlike sprawling network diagrams, the DSM makes coupling positional: modules appear as crisp neighborhoods; problematic loops become targets for deliberate intervention (Browning, 2001).

The same idea spans the triad of architectures. A component–component DSM reveals product structure and points to modular cuts and interface contracts. An activity–activity DSM captures precedence and information flow in processes; by reordering rows and columns, we can minimize uncontrolled iteration and push unavoidable loops into short, managed cycles. A parameter–parameter DSM surfaces analytical coupling for sensitivity and tolerance work, where small changes propagate widely. A people–people DSM exposes where coordination is actually needed so the organization can mirror the technical dependencies it must manage. In practice, component and team DSMs are relatively stable baselines; activity and parameter DSMs are time-based (Eppinger & Browning, 2012; Browning, 2016) (Table 11.1).

Building a DSM is straightforward and iterative. Start by defining the element list at the level you intend to manage—components for a product DSM, activities for a process DSM, teams for an organization DSM. Elicit dependencies (inputs/outputs, constraint links, signals or materials exchanged), optionally noting strength

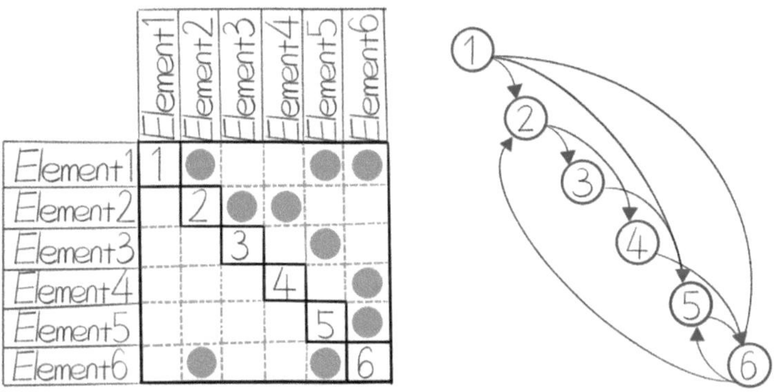

Fig. 11.2 An illustrative DSM and its network representation (Browning, 2016)

Table 11.1 Taxonomy of DSMs

Types	Elements	Applications	Analysis
Static	Component	Product architecting	Clustering
	People/Team	Organization design	Clustering, alignment
Time-based	Activity	Process design	Sequencing, clustering
	Parameter	Low-level process design	Sensitivity, coupling

or criticality. Once drawn, the baseline matrix becomes a design instrument: cluster it to let modules and cores "fall out" of the data and use those clusters to propose subsystem boundaries and the interface rules that will stabilize them; resequence activities to shorten feedback loops and corral the unavoidable ones into tightly time-boxed iterations. Then act on what you see: thin and standardize crossing points, add decouplers or redundancy where propagation risk concentrates, and adjust team boundaries and decision rights so the people who must talk actually do.

The payoffs are concrete. Product architectures become modular by design rather than by slogan: subsystem blocks tighten, interfaces get lighter and more stable, and ad hoc coupling recedes. Process plans grow leaner as hidden loops are surfaced and contained; rework falls and schedules become more predictable. Organizations align with the work: teams cluster around genuine technical neighborhoods, integrators sit at real seams, and selective dual memberships bridge the crossings that matter.

When teams are not arranged to reflect real technical dependencies, coordination overhead grows and defects slip across boundaries; when they are aligned, information flows where the work demands it and changes propagate predictably (Sosa et al., 2004). A DSM makes that alignment—or its absence—explicit and gives designers and managers a concrete basis to reshape product cuts, process sequences, and team structures together. In short, a DSM turns hidden structure into a shared artifact so we can decompose where we must, integrate where we should, and steadily shape the architecture that keeps complex design tractable.

As systems grow in complexity, building and analyzing DSMs by hand becomes costly. LLMs and generative AI can augment the workflow by mining requirements, CAD, code, and test logs to draft element lists, infer dependencies with rationale, and propose initial clusters and sequences that respect both structural signals and natural-language constraints. In large heterogeneous systems, this blend of domain knowledge and mathematical reasoning can surface modular cuts and shorter feedback routes faster than purely heuristic or numerical methods alone. Used this way, generative tools accelerate DSM creation, analysis, and iteration, while the DSM remains the stable, auditable artifact guiding product cuts, process sequencing, and team alignment.

Design Change Propagation

Designs evolve through a constant stream of changes—new requirements, defect fixes, supplier substitutions—and those changes rarely stay local. Because dependencies knit the system together, a tweak in one place can trigger rework elsewhere, slide schedules, and inflate cost. The point is not to eliminate change but to make its pathways visible and manage them deliberately.

A Design Structure Matrix is a natural starting point. By extending each dependency with two judgments—likelihood ("if *j* changes, how likely must *i* change?") and impact ("if *i* changes, how costly or serious is it?")—one can turn a structural picture into a risk-weighted one (Clarkson et al., 2004). This change-prediction framing lets us draw propagation trees that show how a change in one element is expected to ripple through others. The exercise reframes change from surprise into structure: we know where to add tests early, where to place buffers, which interfaces to harden, and which activities to resequence.

Some changes, however, travel along indirect routes or through feedback loops. To capture that, we move beyond single-step dependencies and consider systemic exposure. Using the same DSM, we consider two path-aware indicators for every element: influence and susceptibility (Sarica & Luo, 2019).

- Influence: the total system-wide impact—including on the originator—of a change initiated in a given component, accumulated over all paths.
- Susceptibility: the total impact on a component from changes initiated elsewhere in the system, accumulated over all paths.

These definitions emphasize both directionality and scope. Influence asks, "If this component changes, how much total change will the whole system—including this component—experience?" Susceptibility asks, "How much change will this component absorb due to changes originating anywhere else?" Because these indices account for all routes, including cycles, they surface quiet elements that nevertheless sit on many pathways and quantify how "contagious" a local change may be.

With influence and susceptibility in view, strategy becomes surgical. Components sort into actionable roles: multipliers mainly trigger change, so give them tighter tolerances, added robustness, or architectural decouplers; carriers mainly transmit change, so simplify and stabilize their interfaces, use late binding, and buffer schedules around them; constants sit largely outside propagation, so standardize or freeze them early; absorbers damp incoming change, so keep them simple and highly reliable (Sarica & Luo, 2019). This model-based analysis supports what-if redesign experiments—thin or remove a dependency, strengthen an interface contract, or reorder tasks, then recompute the indices to verify that propagation risk actually drops (Fig. 11.3).

These tools matter because architecture drives propagation. If technical structure routes many dependencies through a few interfaces, those interfaces become leverage points for both improvement and failure; if the process plan hides large feedback loops, rework will surface late; if organizational communication doesn't mirror real technical couplings, issues will ping-pong across boundaries. A change-aware DSM ties these layers together. It connects what can change to how change spreads, and then to who must coordinate. When product interfaces, process sequencing, and team boundaries are adjusted together, changes propagate predictably and cheaply; when they are not, small edits become large problems.

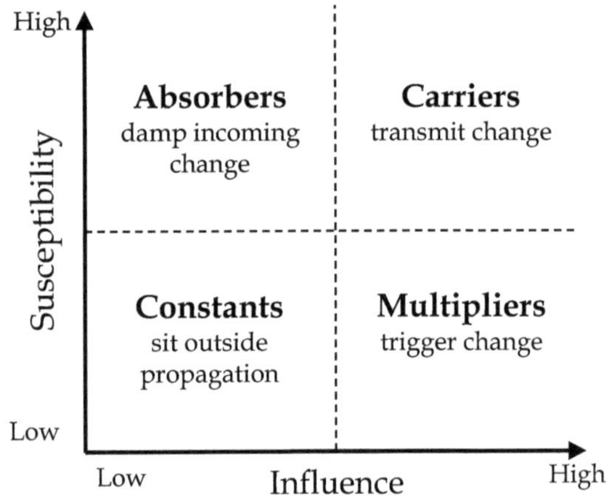

Fig. 11.3 Taxonomy of system components by change propagation profiles (Sarica & Luo, 2019)

The cadence is iterative and light. Start by rating a few critical links for likelihood and impact and sketch the first propagation trees. Use the results to target early tests at high-influence edges and to add slack where susceptibility is high. As evidence accrues, refine the numbers, revisit interface rules, and resequence activities to shorten unavoidable loops. Over time, the system becomes less brittle not because change stops, but because its routes are known and its seams are designed.

Architecture of Co-Design in Ecosystems

Design complexity does not stop at the firm or organization boundary. As products braid hardware, software, services, and infrastructure, the relevant system spans suppliers, complementors, platforms—and sometimes competitors. In this wider arena, architecture becomes an ecosystem property: who depends on whom, through which interfaces, at what cadence. A design that is perfectly manageable inside one company can still falter when inter-firm dependencies are opaque, misaligned, or timed poorly. Seeing and shaping those dependencies is part of design work, not merely corporate strategy (Jacobides et al., 2018).

Modularity, standards, and contracts determine where work gets done. Stable, well-specified interfaces cut transaction costs at module boundaries, letting specialists innovate independently yet integrate predictably. Open interfaces invite diverse suppliers and a rich complement base; tight proprietary ones concentrate control but require stronger orchestration and deeper co-design. Mobile platforms show the trade-off: Android's open architecture spurs device variety and a vast complement ecosystem, while iOS' tighter, curated stack delivers coordinated performance and security. Industries reorganize around these architectural choices—more modularity pushes work to networks of firms; tighter integration pulls it into hierarchical structures with fewer players (Tiwana, 2014; Funk and Luo, 2015).

Healthy ecosystems balance two opposing forces (Baldwin, 2024). Complementarity exerts a centripetal pull: participants must fit together for the whole to work, which favors shared roadmaps, certification, and reference designs. Modularity exerts a centrifugal push: participants can improve their piece without asking permission, which favors autonomy and rapid local innovation. Too little complementarity and the system fragments; too little modularity and it ossifies. Effective ecosystem design stabilizes crossing points—interfaces that are documented, testable, and versioned—while leaving interiors free to evolve.

Technology shapes the feasible balance. Information-dense products with clean separations—think software stacks or cloud services—often admit modular architectures and open ecosystems, where Application Programming Interfaces (APIs) and protocols allow independent teams and firms to move fast. Power-dense, tightly coupled artifacts—think aircrafts or automobiles—tend toward integral architectures that require stronger central coordination because thermal, structural, and dynamic couplings cross subsystem boundaries (Whitney, 1996, 2004). Neither pattern is intrinsically superior. Integral designs are often the shortest path to peak performance and safety where physics couples subsystems strongly; modular designs are often the shortest path to variety, speed, and ecosystem growth where clean interfaces are viable (Baldwin & Clark, 2000; Luo et al., 2012).

For designers, the implication is to co-design the ecosystem alongside the product. Architect thin, stable interfaces so partners can move quickly without constant renegotiation. Align release cadences and compatibility guarantees so external dependencies do not become schedule traps. Decide deliberately what to open to attract complements and what to keep proprietary to sustain advantage—much as platform stewards choose between Android-like openness and iOS-like control. When product structure, process sequencing, and inter-firm governance are designed together, ecosystems amplify innovation rather than amplifying risk.

Design Principles for Managing Complexity

Complexity becomes manageable when teams make structure explicit and pair creativity with disciplined coordination. The aim is not to eliminate complexity, but to shape it—so the system can evolve quickly where it must and remain stable where it should. The principles below translate that stance into day-to-day practice.

Make Structure Visible

Teams map the system at the same grain they intend to manage: components for product, activities for process, and teams for organization. A dependency model such as a DSM turns scattered know-how into a shared artifact. That artifact reveals natural modules, exposes risky crossings, and surfaces hidden feedback loops that leaders can sequence or buffer before they become schedule problems.

Architect Interfaces so Decomposition and Performance Coexist

Designers place integration where the physics demands it and place modularity where variation and learning pay off. Teams define "thin," stable, and testable crossing points, and they write interface contracts that specify both form (signals, geometry, tolerances, protocols) and intent (what matters and how verification will occur). These choices allow subsystems to evolve independently while the whole system performs as intended.

Sequence Work to Reduce Rework

Program leaders treat process architecture with the same rigor they apply to product architecture. They reorder activities to shorten feedback loops, collapse avoidable cycles, and corral unavoidable loops into short, managed iterations. Planners position buffers where they protect the most—at high-susceptibility components and at milestones whose slippage would cascade.

Align the Organization to Real Dependencies

Managers group teams around architectural clusters and give integrators authority and shared budgets at the seams. Coordinators use selective dual memberships or liaison roles where critical work crosses boundaries. These structures reduce handoff friction and ensure that the right people share context at the right interfaces and cadence.

Govern Change Propagation Explicitly

Designers track where changes originate, how far they travel, and what they cost. Teams use influence and susceptibility measures to decide where to harden designs with robustness and decouplers, where to preserve flexibility through options and late binding, and where to deepen tests. A lightweight change forum reviews propagation patterns so local fixes do not become global churn.

Co-design the Ecosystem with the Product

Architects stabilize external interfaces so partners can move without constant renegotiation, and they synchronize release cadences and compatibility guarantees to keep schedules predictable. Leaders decide deliberately what to open to attract complements and what to keep proprietary to sustain advantage, and they revisit those choices as technologies and markets evolve.

Practiced together, these principles turn complexity from an adversary into a design parameter. By seeing structure, shaping interfaces, sequencing work, aligning teams, governing change, and designing with the ecosystem in mind, system designers convert entangled problems into tractable architectures that evolve fast where they must and remain stable where they should.

Making Complexity a Design Material

Complexity is not a foe to defeat but a material to shape. Designers can treat it that way: decompose work to fit human limits, then put performance back at the interfaces through deliberate architecture; make dependencies visible with DSMs; map how change propagates; look beyond the firm to the ecosystem; and apply clear principles in day-to-day practice. Taken together, these moves turn hidden entanglement into legible structure, enabling teams to choose where to integrate tightly, where to modularize, and where to leave room for learning.

Systems thinking gives this approach its coherence and power. By holding product, process, and organization in the same frame—and by tracing feedback, delays, and cross-boundary effects—systems thinking turns architecture from a static blueprint into a living model. Designers use that model to anticipate second-order consequences, to test "what-if" changes before committing, and to align local choices with system outcomes. DSMs, change maps, and ecosystem interfaces become the working instruments of that mindset, while data-driven and AI tools place judgment on firmer ground without replacing it.

Designers, teams, and leaders should treat structure as a first-class design choice. Teams should begin each program by making dependencies explicit. Architects should revisit cuts, seams, and cadences as physics, requirements, or partners shift. Program leaders should pair disciplined interface contracts with clear governance of change. Practiced consistently, these habits turn complexity into leverage: organizations learn faster, integrate cleaner, and deliver systems that evolve quickly where they must and remain stable where they should.

References

Baldwin, C. Y. (2024). *Design rules, volume 2: How technology shapes organizations*. MIT Press.

Baldwin, C. Y., & Clark, K. B. (2000). *Design rules: The power of modularity* (Vol. 1). MIT Press.

Browning, T. R. (2001). Applying the design structure matrix to system decomposition and integration problems: A review and new directions. *IEEE Transactions on Engineering Management, 48*(3), 292–306.

Browning, T. R. (2016). Design structure matrix extensions and innovations: A survey and new opportunities. *IEEE Transactions on Engineering Management, 63*(1), 27–52.

Clarkson, P. J., Simons, C., & Eckert, C. (2004). Predicting change propagation in complex design. *Journal of Mechanical Design, 126*(5), 788–797.

Crawley, E., de Weck, O., Eppinger, S., Magee, C., Moses, J., Seering, W., Schindall, J., Wallace, D., & Whitney, D. (2004). *The influence of architecture in engineering systems* (Engineering Systems Monograph). Massachusetts Institute of Technology.

Eppinger, S. D. (2001). Innovation at the speed of information. *Harvard Business Review, 79*(1), 149–158.

Eppinger, S. D., & Browning, T. R. (2012). *Design structure matrix methods and applications*. MIT Press.

Funk, J., & Luo, J. (2015). Open standards, vertical disintegration and entrepreneurial opportunities: How vertically specialized firms entered the U.S. semiconductor industry. *Technovation, 45–46*, 52–62.

Jacobides, M. G., Cennamo, C., & Gawer, A. (2018). Towards a theory of ecosystems. *Strategic Management Journal, 39*(8), 2255–2276.

Luo, J., Baldwin, C. Y., Whitney, D. E., & Magee, C. L. (2012). The architecture of transaction networks: A comparative analysis of hierarchy in two sectors. *Industrial and Corporate Change, 21*(6), 1307–1335.

Sarica, S., & Luo, J. (2019). An infinite regress model of design change propagation in complex systems. *IEEE Systems Journal, 13*(1), 849–860.

Simon, H. A. (1962). The architecture of complexity. *Proceedings of the American Philosophical Society, 106*(6), 467–482.

Sosa, M. E., Eppinger, S. D., & Rowles, C. M. (2004). The misalignment of product architecture and organizational structure in complex product development. *Management Science, 50*(12), 1674–1689.

Steward, D. V. (1981). The design structure system: A method for managing the design of complex systems. *IEEE Transactions on Engineering Management, 28*(3), 71–74.

Tiwana, A. (2014). *Platform ecosystems: Aligning architecture, governance, and strategy*. Morgan Kaufmann.

Whitney, D. E. (1996). Why mechanical design cannot be like VLSI design. *Research in Engineering Design*, 8(3), 125–138.

Whitney, D. E. (2004). *Physical limits to modularity*. MIT Engineering Systems Division Internal Symposium. MIT DSpace.

Chapter 12
Design and AI

Abstract AI is both material and partner. We show how generative and agentic systems widen search, tighten evidence loops, and scale analysis, prototyping, and evaluation—when embedded with goals, roles, guardrails, and escalation paths. The chapter covers data grounding, verification/validation, bias and safety, provenance from data to decision, and human–AI workflow design. The aim is dependable capability: systems that earn trust through transparency, testing, and governance.

The Innovation Paradox

Designers face an innovation paradox: each wave of progress enlarges the landscape of needs, technologies, and constraints, but human capacity to navigate it does not scale. As prior art deepens, design teams must absorb more knowledge, benchmark more precedents, coordinate across more disciplines, and manage tighter couplings—even as creative cognition remains bounded. Creative AI provides a counterweight by externalizing memory, widening divergence (exploration and generation), and accelerating convergence (evaluation and optimization). The net effect would raise the attainable frontier of design performance and originality (Sarica & Luo, 2024).

AI for Design: Augmenting Core Actions

AI meets design most productively when it amplifies what designers already do—seeing people clearly, generating options boldly, and converging with evidence and speed. The tools differ by task, but the pattern is consistent: AI expands the search where imagination benefits from scale, and it tightens the loop where judgment benefits from fast, structured feedback (Verganti et al., 2020).

It begins with *empathy and opportunity discovery*. Beyond interviews and field notes, AI can listen at scale—sifting reviews, forums, service logs, and usage traces

J. Luo, *Design Science*, Applied Innovation and Technology Management,
https://doi.org/10.1007/978-3-032-13353-3_12

to surface unmet needs and latent segments. Language models cluster and summarize sprawling narratives; anomaly detectors flag pain points that rarely show up in surveys but loom large in behavior. The result is not a replacement for fieldwork but a wider, better map for it—designers enter conversations already primed with hypotheses about who struggles, where, and why.

Translating needs into requirements becomes less lossy when models help carry intent across boundaries. Extractors can propose candidate requirements from qualitative data and trace each back to evidence. Constraint miners gather regulations, standards, and legacy interface rules; consistency checkers spot conflicts and gaps across the stack. Designers remain the arbiters of what matters—but the pipeline from "voice of the user" to "what must be true" grows clearer and faster.

Ideation scales without becoming shapeless when generative models are steered by constraints and precedents. Diffusion, evolutionary search, and LLM-based synthesis can generate many diverse concepts while honoring design envelopes: size, cost, energy, compatibility, brand tone. Retrieval-augmented prompting draws from patents, exemplars, and style guides so novelty builds on knowledge rather than ignoring it. Used this way, AI raises both quantity and quality—not a thousand random sketches, but a curated spread of plausible directions that provoke better human judgment (Luo, 2023).

Prototyping shifts from infrequent leaps to rhythmic, low-cost cycles. Code-generating models turn sketches and flow descriptions into interactive stubs for quick user trials. Generative CAD creates parametric geometry that can be nudged and re-simulated in minutes. Physics-informed surrogates and synthetic data enable "first-order" checks—usability smoke tests, stress or thermal estimates, control stability screens—before teams commit to expensive builds. Evidence arrives earlier, and ideas fail faster and cheaper on their way to something that works.

Evaluation gains tempo when predictions filter the field before high-fidelity testing. Preference models triage concept variants against historical choices and user-stated preferences; performance surrogates approximate expensive simulations and experiments; multi-criteria rankers keep trade-offs explicit rather than buried in a single score. Designers still run real tests—the point is to reserve that budget for the few candidates most likely to pay it back.

Optimization stitches exploration into disciplined convergence. Bayesian optimization and hybrid global–local search steer scarce experiments to informative regions, while constraint handlers enforce feasibility as teams push on performance. Increasingly, agentic orchestration wraps these pieces into a working loop: a planning agent proposes mutations, a simulation agent evaluates, a verifier checks constraints, and a reporter tracks learning—always with humans setting goals, editing prompts, and approving moves.

As systems grow, structure becomes the bottleneck—and here broad-knowledge LLMs help designers make complexity legible. Models can parse requirements, CAD, and code to draft DSM with rationale, and propose initial clusters and task sequences that respect both structural signals and tacit constraints. Classical clustering and ordering algorithms then score and refine those proposals; simulators and

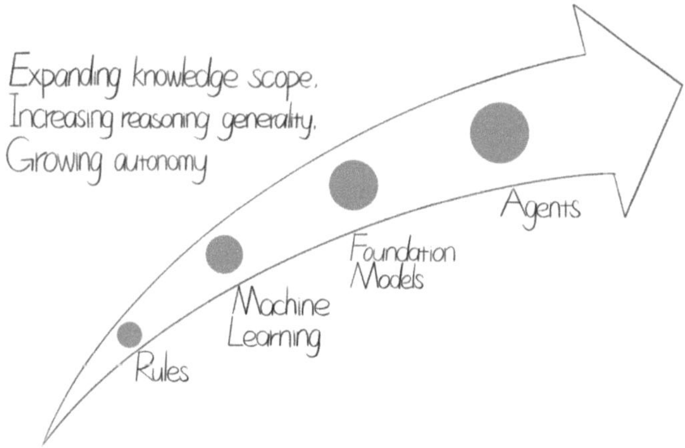

Fig. 12.1 Four waves of AI evolution

data checks verify them. The combination marries AI's breadth and reasoning with mathematical rigor, turning nebulous entanglement into actionable architecture.

None of this replaces craft. AI widens the front end and accelerates the back end; designers supply the aims, the taste, and the ethics. Used deliberately, the result is a studio that looks the same from the outside—people talking to people, drawing, building, testing—but runs on tighter cycles with a wider field of view: more insight going in, more evidence coming out, and more confident choices in between.

The Evolution of AI for Design: Rules → ML → FMs → Agents

AI's role in design has advanced through four discernible waves (Fig. 12.1), each expanding what tools can perceive, reason, and coordinate—and each shifting how designers should integrate them into daily work.

Rules (Expert Systems)

The first wave captured human expertise as explicit if–then rules. In configuration, diagnosis, or tolerance checks, these systems delivered crisp, auditable decisions within narrow domains. Their strength was precision and explainability; their weakness was brittleness. Knowledge engineering was costly, coverage was patchy, and any shift in context required laborious rule maintenance. For design, they acted as guardrails and checklists—useful for enforcing standards and catching contradictions—but they did little to expand the search or adapt to novel problems.

Machine Learning (Task-Specific Models)

The second wave learned from data: classifiers, regressors, and sequence models that predicted preferences, failures, or performance. For design teams, ML became a fast surrogate for expensive tests (e.g., approximating CFD or user choice), a prioritizer for signals in large datasets, and a triage tool for variant screening. These models scaled better than rules and generalized within a task, but they were still narrow: each model solved one problem, demanded labeled data, and required careful retraining as conditions drifted. Integration meant stitching many point tools together—useful, yet orchestration remained a human burden.

Foundation Models (LLMs and Multimodal FMs)

The third wave brought broadly pretrained models with versatile language and reasoning abilities, increasingly coupled with vision, code, and CAD. For design, foundation models (FMs) act as *generalists*: they summarize discovery data, draft requirements with traceable sources, synthesize concepts under constraints, generate code and parametric sketches, and compose experiments around existing tools. Retrieval augmentation grounds their suggestions in priors (patents, standards, corpora), while tool use lets them call solvers and simulators. They expand divergence by proposing diverse, constraint-aware options and speed convergence by structuring evaluation and documentation. Their limitations are equally clear: they can hallucinate, mishandle edge physics, and drift without grounding, so verification layers, provenance, and interface contracts remain essential.

Agents (Agentic and Multi-Agent Systems)

The emerging fourth wave turns models into agents. Agentic systems plan, decompose, and execute multi-step workflows: one agent proposes design mutations; another runs simulations; a third checks constraints and standards; a fourth analyzes results and updates a design log; and a supervisory agent decides whether to continue, branch, or escalate to a human. Multi-agent patterns add specialization (e.g., "requirements agent," "geometry agent," "testing agent") and negotiation protocols to resolve conflicts. In design terms, agents shift value from isolated smart tools to managed loops that iterate autonomously under human goals and governance. The benefits are end-to-end throughput, consistent documentation, and faster learning cycles; the risks are hidden coupling, runaway iterations, and opaque decision paths unless guardrails and audit trails are designed in (Jiang et al., 2025).

Three arcs define the progression. First, knowledge scope grows—from codified local rules to global corpora and cross-modal context. Second, reasoning generality increases—from in-domain pattern use to flexible planning and explanation. Third, orchestration evolves—from human-only stitching to partially autonomous coordination among tools, models, and tests. Each arc demands matching design moves: stronger grounding (e.g., data lineage, retrieval, standards), stronger verification (e.g., simulators, test harnesses, fail-safes), and stronger governance (e.g., versioned prompts, role boundaries, escalation paths) (Verganti et al., 2020).

Choosing "which wave" is situational. If you need high-assurance checks, rules remain powerful and auditable. If you need reliable surrogates or rankers, task-specific ML may be best. If you need breadth—translation across artifacts, rapid ideation, documentation—foundation models shine, provided you ground and verify them. If your bottleneck is orchestration—too many tools, too many handoffs—agentic systems can compress the loop, provided you design clear goals, termination criteria, and human-in-the-loop checkpoints. Across all waves, the system still benefits from the same architectural discipline emphasized in this book: stable interfaces, traceable artifacts, and change governance.

Most design teams will blend waves rather than leapfrog them. Start by instrumenting current workflows (data, tests, decisions). Add foundation models where translation and synthesis are costly (requirements, concepts, reports). Layer ML surrogates where evaluation is the bottleneck. Wrap these capabilities in lightweight agents to plan, execute, and document iterative loops, with humans approving transitions and exceptions. As confidence grows, expand agent autonomy within well-specified envelopes. Throughout, keep a tight coupling to verification and DSM-style structure so the AI-enhanced process remains legible and controllable.

In short, the evolution from rules to agents is not a story of replacement but of envelopment. Each wave subsumes the strengths of the prior while extending the frontier. Designers who pair these capabilities with sound architecture and governance will turn AI from scattered assistance into a coherent, compounding advantage in the design process.

Human–AI Collaboration by Design

Collaboration with AI works best when teams design the relationship on purpose—choosing roles, setting boundaries, and shaping interactions so the system elevates human judgment rather than competing with it (Song et al., 2024). Human designers remain central: they set aims and values, interpret context, make trade-offs, and own accountability, while AI scales search, structure, and speed.

Define Roles and Boundaries

Teams should decide what the AI is for the task—tool, assistant, peer, or coordinator—and they should formalize that role. Leaders should match the role to risk and reversibility: humans retain primacy for safety-critical or irreversible choices, while peer/coordinator modes suit exploratory, fast-iterating work. Teams should make the contract explicit by specifying inputs the AI will consume (requirements, CAD, logs), outputs it must produce (options, analyses, code), quality bars (tests, latency, coverage), and decision rights (what it may propose versus enact). Managers should set escalation paths and stop conditions ("AI proposes → engineer reviews → lead approves") to prevent role drift and to keep accountability clear.

Ground and Verify Outputs

Designers should bind the AI to trusted sources and tools—approved corpora for retrieval, links to solvers and simulators, and access to DSM or requirements systems. So claims remain traceable. Engineers should wrap interactions with checks (units, bounds, compliance) and with verification harnesses that can be rerun. Contributors should require "show-your-work" rationales that include data lineage and constraint satisfaction. Reviewers should calibrate confidence to reality and maintain an audit trail (versioned prompts and logs) so they can reproduce and challenge results.

Design Interaction for Transparency

Teams should shape the collaboration, so the AI adapts detail and pace to user intent and project phase. Interfaces should require the AI to present alternatives and trade-offs rather than a single answer. Designers should treat prompts as interfaces by using templates with constraints, data links, and desired artifacts, plus "explain," "compare," and "challenge" controls that elicit critique. Workflows should present outputs side by side with rationale and quick checks, and they should enable branching and rollback, so exploration proceeds without lock-in.

Govern and Adapt the Partnership

Leads should allocate tasks explicitly, define handoffs, and set termination criteria (e.g., stop after N loops or after diminishing returns). Security owners should gate sensitive actions with permission, and reliability owners should schedule red-team drills to probe failure modes. Program managers should measure the partnership—throughput, quality, exploration breadth, and learning—and they should revise roles, prompts, and guardrails as evidence accumulates. Governance should let autonomy expand within safe envelopes when performance proves out and contract when drift or novelty appears.

Table 12.1 Design principles for human–AI collaboration

Design principles	Action guidelines
Define roles & boundaries	Name the AI's role (tool/assistant/peer/coordinator), match autonomy to risk and reversibility, and codify inputs, outputs, quality bars, decision rights, and escalation paths
Ground & verify outputs	Bind the AI to trusted data and tools; require provenance and "show-your-work"; wrap results with rerunnable checks and simulators
Design for transparency	Make prompts into interfaces; surface alternatives, assumptions, and trade-offs; enable easy branching and rollback
Govern & adapt	Allocate tasks and handoffs; set termination criteria and permissions; expand autonomy within safe envelopes and contract it on drift
Build & maintain trust	Treat trust as a workflow property; calibrate confidence; publish limits; run red-team drills; provide user controls (opt-outs, kill switches, granular permissions)

Build and Maintain Trust

Teams should treat trust as a workflow property, not a feeling. Designers should build trust with verification (tests, simulators, and checks around AI outputs), provenance (links to data, standards, and prior decisions), and accountability (logs, versioned prompts, reproducible runs). Reviewers should calibrate model confidence to reality, and authors should require "show-your-work" rationales and hedging when evidence is weak. Risk owners should publish known limitations and domain bounds, run periodic red-team drills to surface failure modes, and provide user control—opt-outs, kill switches, and granular permissions—so decisions remain contestable and confidence stays earned and appropriately bounded.

Done well, human–AI collaboration becomes a disciplined practice: human designers hold purpose, values, and final accountability; AI extends reach and tempo by scaling search and structure; and the joint system learns in public—faster when it can, slower when it should. The payoff is not only speed but clarity: shared context improves, reasoning stays transparent, and decisions remain traceable as designs grow in scope and consequence. Clear roles, grounded outputs, transparent interactions, adaptive governance, and engineered trust are the levers that transform AI from a clever tool into a reliable partner at scale (Table 12.1).

Design for AI: Creativity, Ethics, and Value

Designing with AI changes how teams work; designing for AI changes what teams build. Treat AI systems as complex, evolving artifacts whose behavior emerges from representations, data, interfaces, and governance. The creative act is twofold: invent mechanisms that make AI useful, and shape the social contract that makes it acceptable.

Contemporary AI models embody designed ideas by analogy: neural networks draw on neuroscience's distributed representation (many simple units encoding rich structure); attention borrows a psychological insight by weighting what matters when it matters; diffusion adopts a physics metaphor, iteratively denoising randomness into form. Crucially, these are not natural laws but human creative choices—how we represent problems, set objectives and constraints, curate data, combine architectures, and stage training and feedback. Those choices determine what the system can notice, generate, and ignore; they define its limits as much as its strengths. Treating AI as designed keeps creativity in the foreground: designers decide what the model should care about, how it trades off goals, and how people will steer, verify, and override it in use.

AI capability becomes a product only when designers make it legible, steerable, and safe. Interfaces must expose intent. Feedback should explain trade-offs. Controls need to modulate behavior. Good experiences help users think with the model: they present alternatives side by side, make assumptions and sources visible, and keep paths reversible so exploration feels safe. Teams should treat prompts, constraints, and datasets as first-class design materials, and they should instrument those materials for inspection and reuse.

Ethical aspirations become real only when teams operationalize them. Workflows must embed fairness, transparency, and accountability rather than relegating them to an end-of-project document. Designers should encode use constraints (who/what/when), track data lineage and consent, require explanations proportionate to risk, and maintain an auditable trail from requirement to release. Reviews should pair quantitative checks (bias metrics, subgroup performance, robustness tests) with qualitative assessments (impacted-user walkthroughs, scenario red-teaming). Publishers need to state known limitations and fallback behaviors. Products should provide user agency—opt-outs, kill switches, and selectable decision policies—so people can contest outcomes and choose acceptable levels of automation. Responsible AI becomes an ongoing design relationship between system and society, not a checklist (Karekezi et al., 2025).

AI systems change as data, models, and contexts shift. Architects should design for controlled evolution by modularizing the stack (data → features → models → policies → interfaces) with versioned contracts at each seam. Organizations should separate capability from policy: the model can do many things, while the governance layer decides what it may do here and now. Teams ought to use shadow deployments and staged rollouts to measure impact before broad release. Verification harnesses should be runnable across versions, and reference scenarios should be frozen so regressions are visible. Monitoring must be part of the product: it should track drift, harm signals, and user overrides, and it should feed actionable signals into the change process.

Performance matters, but value lives in fit. Programs should measure the speed of learning loops, the cost to reach evidence, the reduction of coordination friction, the reliability of handoffs, and the degree to which the system expands human capability without eroding trust. Teams should define success with multi-objective metrics—user outcomes, equity impacts, total cost of ownership, maintainability, and time-to-adapt when requirements change—and they should link these metrics to business and societal goals so trade-offs are explicit. Decision-makers should recognize that a slightly more accurate model that is harder to govern or adapt may destroy value, while a slightly less accurate model that is more legible and tunable may unlock it.

Designers should approach AI not as a magical oracle but as a designed, socio-technical system. Projects should start from human purpose, choose mechanisms that align with that purpose, and make constraints and consequences explicit. Interfaces should stay thin and testable so partners—and future teams—can build on the work. Teams should maintain humility about uncertainty and bake learning into the lifecycle by planning the next experiment, the next audit, and the next conversation with affected users. Designing for AI becomes continuous architecture: it shapes mechanisms, interactions, and norms so intelligence serves human aims—and keeps earning its place in the systems people live with.

Designing for AI asks designers to shape both mechanism and meaning. The work is creative (choosing representations, objectives, data, and architectures), experiential (making capabilities legible, steerable, and safe), responsible (operationalizing fairness, transparency, and accountability), architectural (building systems that can evolve under control), and value-focused (optimizing fit, not just accuracy). Treated this way, AI becomes a socio-technical product that learns without losing accountability, innovates without eroding trust, and delivers durable value (Table 12.2).

Table 12.2 Design-for-AI principles and guidelines

Design principles	Action guidelines
Design the mechanism	Choose representations, objectives, constraints, data, and architecture deliberately; make those design choices explicit and reviewable
Turn capability into experience	Expose intent, surface trade-offs, and provide controls; present alternatives with rationale and keep exploration reversible
Operationalize responsibility	Encode use constraints, track data lineage and consent, require explanations proportionate to risk, and audit decisions end-to-end
Evolve under control	Modularize the stack with versioned contracts; separate capability from policy; use shadow/staged rollouts and reusable verification harnesses
Monitor and respond	Instrument drift, harm signals, and user overrides; route those signals into a disciplined change process
Measure value, not just accuracy	Track time-to-evidence, coordination friction, reliability of handoffs, adaptability, user outcomes, equity impacts, and total cost of ownership
Keep interfaces thin and testable	Prefer stable, documented contracts so partners and future teams can build, test, and replace components safely

Toward a Symbiotic Human–AI Design Ethos

Designers now work in a landscape where AI is both material to shape and partner to collaborate with (Fig. 12.2). Effective human–AI symbiosis rests on systemic design moves: explicit role partitioning, legible interface contracts, guardrails and governance, provenance and auditability, and continuous co-evolution. Creative AI widens search while tightening loops, so designers can explore farther and converge faster; but the gains arrive only when these decisions—aims, constraints, verification, and governance—are made explicit and designed into the workflow. Building on the earlier chapters' emphasis on decomposition, architecture, and disciplined convergence, this chapter extends the stance to AI itself: designers should architect AI into the process with clear roles, legible interfaces, and auditable paths from data to decision.

The tools will keep evolving—from rules to task-specific ML, to foundation models, to agentic systems—but the design stance remains stable. Designers should pair breadth with grounding, autonomy with oversight, and speed with evidence. Human judgment must continue to hold the line on meaning, values, and trade-offs, while AI scales pattern finding, synthesis, prototyping, evaluation, and optimization. When teams treat collaboration as a designed workflow—transparent, testable, and revisable—they convert algorithmic capability into dependable capability.

Finally, the opportunity is not only better performance but better AI systems: systems that learn without losing accountability, innovate without eroding trust, and evolve without collapsing under their own complexity. Designers who keep architecture, ethics, and values in view will raise the attainable frontier of originality and performance—and do so in a way that remains legible to the people those systems serve.

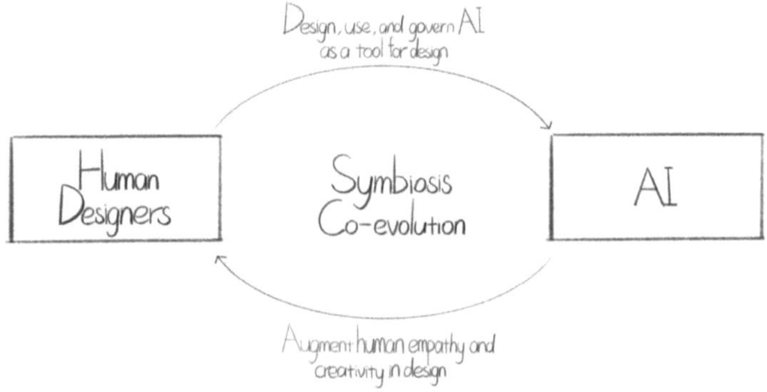

Fig. 12.2 Human–AI Symbiosis and Co-evolution in Design

References

Jiang, S., Xie, M., Chen, Y., Ma, J., & Luo, J. (2025). Intelligent Design 4.0: Paradigm evolution toward the agentic AI era. arXiv:2506.09755.

Karekezi, P., Moore, G., & Luo, J. (2025). Human-centered AI design: Developers' perspectives. *Journal of Engineering Design*, 1–16. https://doi.org/10.1080/09544828.2025.2518907

Luo, J. (2023). Data-driven innovation: What is it? *IEEE Transactions on Engineering Management, 70*(2), 784–797.

Sarica, S., & Luo, J. (2024). The innovation paradox: Concept-space expansion with diminishing originality and the promise of creative artificial intelligence. *Design Science, 10*, e11.

Song, B., Zhu, Q., & Luo, J. (2024). Human–AI collaboration by design. In *Proceedings of the Design Society: 18th International Design Conference (DESIGN 2024), Cavtat, Dubrovnik, Croatia.*

Verganti, R., Vendraminelli, L., & Iansiti, M. (2020). Innovation and design in the age of artificial intelligence. *Journal of Product Innovation Management, 37*(3), 212–227.

Chapter 13
Design for X

Abstract Design extends beyond artifacts to outcomes. We develop "Design for X" across business (value capture and models), entrepreneurship (venture as designed system), public policy (legitimacy, equity, implementation), and sustainability (United Nations SDGs - Sustainable Development Goalscircularity, life-cycle thinking). Methods include outcome-level requirements, market and policy experiments, and systems metrics (e.g., carbon, inclusion). The chapter turns "for X" into a method: creativity expansive, consequences legible, and adjustable.

X as Outcome Architecture

Design does not end at the artifact. A concept that delights in the lab can stall in the market, falter as a venture, collide with public rules, or create hidden social, economic, and ecological costs at scale (United Nations, 2015). "Design for X" names the shift from crafting things to shaping outcomes—business models that capture value, ventures that can adapt and grow, policies that earn legitimacy and equity, and performance that respects sustainability. The work remains design, but the unit of analysis widens: from features and forms to value flows, organizational and public institutions, and life-cycle consequences.

Thinking this way reframes requirements. Instead of asking only "What must the product do?," designers also ask "What must the outcome do—for customers, for the business, for citizens and society, and for the biosphere?" These requirements-of-outcomes become explicit objectives and constraints: willingness-to-pay and unit economics for business; safety, equity, and compliance for public policy; embodied carbon and circularity for sustainability. Once named, they can be modeled, traded off, prototyped, and verified with the same discipline applied to geometry, tolerance, or code.

This stance extends—and depends on—earlier principles. Empathy still anchors the work, now spanning users, customers, citizens, frontline officials, and affected communities. Ontology still supplies the shared vocabulary that makes problems

J. Luo, *Design Science*, Applied Innovation and Technology Management,
https://doi.org/10.1007/978-3-032-13353-3_13

and options computable, while ideation and creativity generate variety across offerings, business models, policy instruments, and circular pathways. Prototyping still reduces uncertainty—via MVPs and market experiments, policy pilots and sandboxes, and life-cycle trials—while convergence still makes choices, balancing desirability, feasibility, viability, legitimacy, and sustainability through controlled convergence and optimization. Architecture still governs behavior across product, process, organization, channels, agencies, partners, and supply chains; DSMs still reveal where risk and rework concentrate. And AI still partners with designers—widening search, drafting business and policy options, grounding decisions in evidence, and tightening feedback loops as outcomes scale.

This chapter focuses on four Xs—among many designers may face. Design for business treats value as an architectural choice—who benefits, who pays, and how revenue and cost structures support scale. Design for entrepreneurship treats the venture itself as a socio-technical artifact—adaptively partitioned, tested, and re-cut under uncertainty and resource constraints. Design for public policy treats legitimacy and equity as designed properties—what instruments governments combine, how implementation is governed across agencies and partners, and how evidence and accountability stay in the loop for citizens. Design for sustainability adopts the UN SDG sense—spanning environmental, social, and economic dimensions—so materials, energy, labor, inclusion, and livelihoods are designed across the life cycle, not audited afterward. Taken together, these perspectives turn "for X" from a slogan into a method—keeping creativity expansive while making consequences legible, measurable, and adjustable.

Design for Business

Design for business treats value as an architectural choice. A product can create immense value yet capture little if the system cut—who owns which modules, where interfaces are thin or thick, who pays whom, and on what terms—leaves surplus to others. A thoughtful partition, by contrast, can translate invention into durable profit. The design task is to pair a value proposition that someone will pay for with a value-capture plan that survives competition.

Capturing value begins by distinguishing "who benefits" from "who pays." It requires a defensible position in the value chain and assets rivals cannot cheaply copy—distinctive know-how and routines, privileged data or locations, or control points where performance is bottlenecked (Teece, 1986). When those assets are sticky and scarce, margins persist; when they are generic and mobile, value leaks to partners or customers.

Architecture determines where value accumulates. One effective pattern is to own the performance bottleneck—the integral module that sets the system's ceiling—while opening complements to attract partners and variety (Baldwin & Clark, 2000).

Outsourced complements can vary without harming the whole if the bottleneck dominates outcomes. A DSM view of the product and value chain clarifies what to integrate, what to modularize, and where to place interface contracts so bargaining power does not drift away (Henderson & Clark, 1990).

Openness is a design variable. Opening interfaces can create more total value by engaging outside talent, reducing in-house problem solving, and accelerating adoption, while closing key modules preserves bargaining power where differentiation, safety, or liability demand tight control (Funk & Luo, 2015). Platform choices—APIs, SDKs (Software Development Kits), certification, versioning—tune this balance: open where network effects and complements matter; close where system integrity and distinctiveness depend on it (Parker et al., 2016). Mobile ecosystems illustrate the range: broadly open architectures grow complements and reach, while tighter stacks concentrate control and deliver coordinated performance and security. The "right" openness follows where effects sit, which side you must subsidize, and which module you must control to keep options open.

Business model design—pricing, metering (one-time, usage, subscription), bundling, and channel strategy—belongs to the same architectural cut, not afterthoughts (Osterwalder & Pigneur, 2010). Teams treat these choices like design variables: they run controlled convergence on model variants against willingness-to-pay, margin structure, cash-flow timing, and sensitivity to scale, churn, and support costs. They prototype offers, read cohort curves and payback period in context, and refine the model as they would an interface—letting evidence, not attachment, drive the next iteration.

In many categories, architecture includes services as well as artifacts. Product–service systems (PSS) are a social technical design choice that treats offerings as product-plus-service bundle (or service delivered through assets) to create and capture value (Tukker, 2004; Baines et al., 2007). Service layers (installation, monitoring, upgrades, financing) add value in use and enable subscriptions, usage/outcome-based contracts, and data-enabled services beyond unit sales. PSS shifts revenue to performance over time, aligning incentives with durability, maintainability, telemetry, and serviceable interfaces; thus the architectural cut must include service interfaces, roles, and partner networks—not just artifact modules.

Intellectual property is a lever, not a lifeboat. Patents can buy time to build complementary assets and slow fast followers; secrecy can protect know-how where enforcement is weak. Both are means to an architectural end: protect the bottleneck if law is strong, open complements to attract developers, and use time-to-market and learning as moats where law is weak.

Designing for business means positioning the bottleneck you must own—across product and service layers—choosing openness where complements drive adoption, and selecting a revenue model that aligns incentives across the chain. Teams treat the business model and service architecture as part of the system architecture—prototype them, instrument with evidence, and iterate with the same discipline applied to technical design (Table 13.1).

Table 13.1 Design-for-business principles

Design principles	Action guidelines
Own the bottleneck	Keep the performance-defining module integral to anchor bargaining power
Cut the system deliberately	Place interfaces where variation pays; hold tight control where integrity/ safety demand it
Tune openness	Open complements to grow value; close differentiators to retain capture (APIs/SDKs, versioned contracts)
Architect the business model	Treat pricing, metering, bundling, and channels as design variables; prototype and iterate
Bundle product and service	Treat the offering as product-plus-service; tie revenue to performance over time; co-design service interfaces, telemetry, and partner roles alongside artifact modules.
Let evidence lead	Compare models via controlled convergence on WTP, margin structure, payback period, churn
Use IP as a lever	Protect the bottleneck where law is strong; rely on speed/learning where it isn't
Align incentives	Ensure partners, channels, and customers benefit when core economics improve
Instrument for learning	Tie product metrics to unit economics and value capture with dashboards

Design for Entrepreneurship

Design for entrepreneurship treats a venture as a holistic socio-technical system, adaptively designed and built under extreme uncertainty and tight resources. Founders act as system architects: they decide how to partition the problem, what to test first, how to absorb learning, and when to re-cut the architecture as evidence accumulates. In that sense, entrepreneurs are socio-technical system designers.

Founding teams are the first architecture to design. Teams blend skills, networks, and working norms under a shared value system. Close ties bring trust but raise the stakes of conflict, while homophily eases communication but narrows perspective. Equity functions as incentive and governance: vesting, cliffs, and milestone triggers align future contribution with ownership and preserve options when uncertainty is highest.

Under uncertainty, speed to evidence beats speed to artifact. Pretotypes "fake it before you make it" to test behavior and demand with minimal build; MVPs instrument core hypotheses with paying early adopters, turning anecdotes into metrics, and narrowing the credible model space. Each loop ends with a decision—pivot, persevere, or park—so learning compounds and burn stays purposeful (Blank & Dorf, 2012).

Flexibility is crucial in volatile markets, but it is not free; ventures pay for it in architecture, interfaces, and parts. Teams modularize where variation is likely, decouple interfaces, reduce unique parts, and leave allowances around likely-to-change modules. Platforming converts parallel variants into options the venture can exercise if the world moves that way; option value rises with uncertainty, so design where uncertainty lives.

Bootstrapping is design method. Capital constraints become design prompts: advance payments and pre-orders validate demand; shared facilities and creative partnerships reduce burn; targeted experiments replace grand launches. As evidence

Table 13.2 Design-for-entrepreneurship principles

Design principles	Action guidelines
Design the team first	Staff for complementary skills/values; treat equity as evolving governance (vesting, cliffs, milestones)
Prioritize speed to evidence	Run pretotypes/MVPs; end each loop with pivot-persevere-park decisions
Place flexibility where it pays	Modularize likely-to-change areas; decouple interfaces; keep option value high
Bootstrap deliberately	Use pre-orders, shared facilities, and partnerships to reduce burn before raising capital
Scale ambidextrously	Preserve exploration paths alongside reliable delivery; redraw boundaries as dependencies shift
Use AI as elastic staff	Offload search, analysis, and orchestration—with grounding, verification, and governance
Measure what matters	Track learning rate, traction, payback period, and burn; adjust architecture accordingly
Treat the venture as an artifact	Re-architect product, process, and organization as evidence accumulates

accumulates—customers, unit economics, repeatability—external capital becomes a catalyst, not a crutch (McGrath & MacMillan, 1995).

Scaling introduces hierarchy and the risk of rigidity. Ambidextrous structures preserve a "special forces" path for exploration alongside stable delivery paths for exploitation (O'Reilly & Tushman, 2004). As product and ecosystem architectures evolve, leaders redraw team boundaries to track real dependencies, grant integrators authority where coupling is tight, and preserve short, reversible paths for experimentation.

Modern founders also use LLMs and agents as elastic staff: mining opportunity signals, drafting offers and pricing narratives, composing experiments, analyzing telemetry, and coordinating toolchains. The same systems support business-architecture choices—where to place the bottleneck, how to open interfaces without losing control—by scanning prior art and simulating scenarios. Grounding, verification, and governance turn that assistance into reliable leverage.

Designing for entrepreneurship means running fast, frugal, instrumented loops that convert uncertainty into knowledge and knowledge into traction. Entrepreneurial teams continuously re-architect the product-process-organization triad to reflect what you learn, treating the venture as an evolving artifact and allowing the business model to converge with the design (Table 13.2).

Design for Public Policy

Design for public policy treats government action as a deliberate, evidence-seeking design process. Policymakers and public designers specify aims, translate those aims into constraints and metrics, and compose instruments into workable bundles. The artifacts are not only documents and laws; they are programs, service experiences, data pipelines, and accountability mechanisms that must operate in the open and at scale. The central question is not "What rule can we write?" but "What behavior should the system produce, for whom, at what cost, and with what safeguards?"

Public designers begin with outcomes, not tools. Teams name the objectives, such as safety, equity, resilience, growth, and express them in measurable terms. Teams also acknowledge the multi-objective nature of policy: a clean energy subsidy should reduce emissions, protect vulnerable ratepayers, and preserve grid stability; a mobility rule should improve access without pricing out essential trips. When teams make trade-offs explicit, they can ideate, prototype, test, and refine without hiding value judgments.

Policy instruments form a modular toolkit (Hood, 1983), and designers treat them that way. Legislatures and agencies can choose among standards and bans, disclosure and labeling, taxes and subsidies, tradable permits, procurement, liability regimes, and "nudges" embedded in choice architecture. Designers can combine instruments into policy bundles that are more robust than any single lever (Howlett & Rayner, 2007). A building-efficiency standard, for example, can pair with procurement of low-carbon materials, incentives for retrofits, and mandatory data disclosure, so each instrument supports the others and closes predictable loopholes.

Implementation architecture determines whether a good policy design survives contact with reality. Agencies, municipalities, regulated firms, civil society groups, and vendors must coordinate across seams. Designers can map these dependencies with the same discipline used for complex products: a "policy DSM" makes visible who depends on whose data, whose approvals unlock which steps, and where change will propagate if a regulation, budget, or platform shifts (Eppinger, 2001). Program leaders can then align decision rights, interfaces, and cadence across agencies; place integrators at high-coupling seams; and thin crossing points so handoffs become reliable rather than fragile.

Evidence and legitimacy grow together when teams prototype policies. Policymakers can use pilots, regulatory sandboxes, staged rollouts, and sunset clauses to convert hypotheses into measurements. Designers can instrument these trials with outcome and distributional metrics, so they observe not only average effects but also who benefits, who bears costs, and where harms concentrate. Public design teams should publish the criteria for continuation, expansion, or repeal in advance, so the public can see how evidence links to decisions.

Measurement makes policy governable. Teams should define indicators for compliance, outcomes, and unintended consequences, and they should assign owners who will monitor, explain, and act. Designers can pair quantitative checks with qualitative review: participatory walkthroughs with affected communities, scenario red-teaming with independent experts, and open "after-action" reports when policies miss. These practices turn accountability from a threat into a capability.

AI now extends policy design without replacing judgment. Retrieval-grounded synthesis can surface precedent across jurisdictions; large models can draft options, summarize comments, and map conflicts among stakeholder submissions; agentic workflows can run "generate-simulate-verify" loops with microsimulations or agent-based models to explore consequence space before rules go live. Designers

Table 13.3 Design-for-policy principles

Design principles	Action guidelines
Start from outcomes	Define multi-objective goals (effectiveness, equity, resilience); make trade-offs explicit
Compose instruments	Combine standards, incentives, disclosure, procurement, and liability into coherent bundles
Architect implementation	Map inter-agency/partner dependencies (policy DSM); place integrators at tight seams
Prototype in public	Use pilots, sandboxes, staged rollouts, sunset clauses; pre-commit decision criteria
Measure and adapt	Track compliance, outcomes, unintended effects; assign owners and act on signals
Build legitimacy	Write plainly; provide contestation paths; ensure accessibility and multilingual support
Ground with evidence & AI	Use retrieval-grounded synthesis, simulation, and agents with provenance and review
Document accountability	Maintain auditable trails from requirement to release; publish limits and updates

should bind these tools to trusted corpora, require provenance for claims, and route sensitive steps through human review. Used this way, AI increases search breadth and speeds analysis while keeping legitimacy anchored in transparent reasoning.

Equity and trust remain design properties, not afterthoughts. Teams should require accessible language in communications, multilingual interfaces in services, and assistive alternatives for those without digital access. Programs should publish "known limitations" and fallback behaviors so the public knows what to expect when systems fail. Agencies should create contestation paths—appeals, ombudspersons, and human escalation—for decisions that materially affect people's rights or livelihoods. These mechanisms do not slow policy; they make it durable.

Design for public policy, done rigorously, looks like good engineering with public values in the loop. Teams start from outcomes, choose and combine instruments, architect implementation across institutions, prototype and measure in the open, and adapt as evidence accumulates. When designers treat the state as a socio-technical system, the work shifts from issuing static rules to shaping evolvable programs that learn, correct, and earn trust over time (Table 13.3).

Design for Sustainability

Design for sustainability treats environmental and social performance as first-class design objectives, not post hoc audits. Teams specify what "good" means across the life cycle—extraction, manufacturing, logistics, use, service, and end-of-life—and across people and places affected by those flows. The central question is not "How green is this part?" but "How do materials, energy, money, and harms/benefits move through the system, and how do we change the architecture so value rises while impact and inequity fall?"

Teams begin by defining objectives and scope. Designers choose which impact categories matter—greenhouse gases, water, land, toxicity, occupational health and safety, fair labor, living wages, diversity and inclusion, accessibility, data privacy, and community impact—and they set system boundaries that match decisions they can influence. Product teams often start with cradle-to-gate scope to clean up upstream impacts, then expand to cradle-to-grave or cradle-to-cradle as they tackle use and recovery. Clear scope prevents "impact leakage," where improvements shift burdens to other communities or life-cycle stages.

Architecture shapes sustainability because it shapes flow. Designers can map the life cycle with a DSM for flows: each node is a stage (supplier tiers, plants, distribution, use, service, recovery), and each link represents material, energy, information, and labor dependency. This makes hotspots visible—energy-intensive steps, fragile single-source materials, unsafe processes, wage pressure points, data-risk handoffs—and exposes where design changes will propagate. Teams then place decouplers (material substitutions, shared subassemblies, standardized fasteners), buffers (remanufacturing pools, safety stock at risk nodes), and tests (incoming quality, carbon and wage audits, privacy compliance) at the seams that matter.

Modularity is a lever for circularity and inclusion. Designers create repairable and upgradeable products by separating high-wear or high-obsolescence modules from long-lived structures; they use accessible fasteners, repair-friendly packaging, and diagnostic interfaces to lower service friction for end users and independent repairers (Ellen MacArthur Foundation, 2015). Where physics demands integral architectures, teams concentrate circular strategies in peripherals (replaceable skins, batteries, control boards) and design safe, ergonomic service procedures that reduce injury risk. The goal is not maximal modularity but targeted modularity where it unlocks reuse, remanufacture, recycling, and safer work.

Measurement turns aspiration into action. Teams run life-cycle assessment (LCA) for environmental factors and pair it with social LCA or supplier scorecards (injury rates, wage benchmarks, hours, grievance mechanisms, demographic representation). They publish Environmental Product Declarations (EPDs) where markets demand them, track embodied carbon, water intensity, and critical minerals, and monitor social indicators (e.g., ISO 45001 conformance, living-wage coverage, accessibility scores, privacy incidents). Engineers use multi-objective optimization to trade off impact, performance, cost, and social metrics: small geometry or process changes can cut mass, eliminate hazardous steps, reduce takt-time strain, and lower exposure to solvents or heat.

Business models either enable or block sustainability and equity. Product-as-a-service, long warranties, and buyback programs create incentives to design for durability, maintainability, recovery, and fair service work (Bocken et al., 2014). Platformed components simplify logistics and reduce inventory waste; tiered pricing or public–private partnerships can improve access for underserved users. Deposit schemes, take-back logistics, and right-to-repair policies close loops that would otherwise remain aspirational.

Supply chains determine feasibility. Teams build traceability (material passports, batch certificates), standards (recycled content, repairability, accessibility), and certification (responsible minerals, fair labor, low-carbon processes) so claims are verifiable and procurement is repeatable (Gawer & Cusumano, 2014). Many programs need dual strategies: near-term improvements with current suppliers and longer term shifts to new processes or regions to reduce both environmental risk and social vulnerability. The life-cycle DSM helps identify single points of failure—technical or human—and guides diversification or redesign.

Policy can accelerate and anchor progress. Designers align with regulations on durability, repairability, chemicals, extended producer responsibility, modern-slavery reporting, and accessibility. Early engagement with certifiers and regulators helps shape realistic tests and avoids late redesigns. Public procurement and standardized disclosures reward low-impact, high-equity solutions and reduce the cost of doing the right thing.

AI can speed sustainable design without replacing judgment. Models can mine supplier disclosures, bills of materials, and human resources and safety data to estimate footprints and flag hotspots quickly; surrogates can approximate LCA and social-risk responses for early exploration; and generative tools can propose lower impact form factors, routings, or materials under environmental and social constraints. Agentic loops can run generate-simulate-verify cycles that screen thousands of variants for impact, cost, ergonomics, and compliance, then route finalists to human review. Teams keep these systems grounded with audited datasets, documented assumptions, and verification harnesses so suggestions remain trustworthy.

Design for sustainability, done rigorously, looks like good systems engineering with the planet and people in the loop. Teams define outcomes and scope, map flows, re-cut the architecture where it unlocks circularity and safety, and couple LCA/social metrics with optimization and business-model choices. Organizations align supply, policy, and service so improvements survive contact with reality and reach the communities that need them. When designers treat the environment and society as boundary conditions—and the life cycle as a design space—products become easier to maintain, businesses become more resilient and inclusive, and impacts decline in ways that compound over time (Table 13.4).

Table 13.4 Design-for-sustainability principles

Design principles	Action guidelines
Broaden the brief	Treat environmental and social impacts as first-class objectives across the life cycle
Set the boundary	Choose cradle-to-gate/grave/circle scopes; avoid impact leakage across stages/communities
Map flows	Build a life-cycle DSM (materials, energy, information, labor); locate hotspots and propagation
Target modularity	Enable repair, upgrade, and recovery where it counts; design safe, ergonomic service
Measure and optimize	Pair LCA with social metrics; run multi-objective optimization (impact, cost, performance)
Align the model	Use warranties, take-back, product-as-a-service, deposits to make circularity viable
Harden the chain	Build traceability, standards, certification; diversify technical and human single points of failure
Leverage policy & AI	Anticipate regulation; use models/agents to explore low-impact variants with audited data

From Artifact to Outcome

Design for X reframes the work: the unit of design is not only the product, but the outcomes it makes possible—value that endures, ventures that learn and scale, policies that earn legitimacy, and impacts that remain within social and planetary bounds. Across business, entrepreneurship, public policy, and sustainability, the method is the same. Designers widen the brief to include the right objectives and constraints, make dependencies visible, and shape architectures—of products, processes, organizations, and ecosystems—so consequences are legible, measurable, and adjustable. Creativity still leads, but it is coupled to disciplined convergence; ideas are many, evidence is tight, and choices are traceable.

The tools from earlier chapters carry this work. Empathy broadens to citizens and communities; ontology keeps options computable; ideation explores not just form but business models, instruments, and circular pathways; prototyping moves from MVPs to policy pilots and life-cycle trials; optimization balances cost, performance, equity, and footprint; architecture and DSMs align teams with real dependencies; change-propagation analysis prevents small edits from becoming large problems. AI now scales search and structure, drafts alternatives, grounds judgments in precedent, and accelerates learning loops—yet human purpose and accountability remain the frame.

What "for X" finally offers is a stance: treat outcomes as designed. Start from the ends you seek; choose system cuts that place control where it matters; instrument the path so learning compounds; and revisit decisions as evidence and context evolve. Done this way, design stops at neither the drawing nor the launch. It becomes continuous architecture—of mechanisms and institutions, of incentives and interfaces—so the things we make are aligned with the futures we intend.

References

Baines, T. S., Lightfoot, H. W., Evans, S., Neely, A., Greenough, R., Peppard, J., et al. (2007). State-of-the-art in product-service systems. Proceedings of the Institution of Mechanical Engineers, Part B: *Journal of Engineering Manufacture*, 221(10), 1543–1552.

Baldwin, C. Y., & Clark, K. B. (2000). *Design rules, volume 1: The power of modularity*. MIT Press.

Blank, S., & Dorf, B. (2012). *The startup owner's manual*. K&S Ranch.

Bocken, N. M. P., Short, S. W., Rana, P., & Evans, S. (2014). A literature and practice review of sustainable business model archetypes. *Journal of Cleaner Production, 65*, 42–56.

Ellen MacArthur Foundation. (2015). *Towards the circular economy*. Ellen MacArthur Foundation.

Eppinger, S. D. (2001). Innovation at the speed of information. *Harvard Business Review, 79*(1), 149–158.

Gawer, A., & Cusumano, M. A. (2014). Industry platforms and ecosystem innovation. *Journal of Product Innovation Management, 31*(3), 417–433.

Henderson, R. M., & Clark, K. B. (1990). Architectural innovation: The reconfiguration of existing product technologies and the failure of established firms. *Administrative Science Quarterly, 35*(1), 9–30.

Hood, C. (1983). *The tools of government*. Macmillan.

Howlett, M., & Rayner, J. (2007). Design principles for policy mixes: Cohesion and coherence in 'new governance arrangements'. *Policy and Society, 26*(4), 1–18.

Funk, J., & Luo, J. (2015). Open standards, vertical disintegration and entrepreneurial opportunities: How vertically specialized firms entered the U.S. semiconductor industry. *Technovation, 45–46*, 52–62.

McGrath, R. G., & MacMillan, I. C. (1995). Discovery-driven planning. *Harvard Business Review, 73*(4), 44–54.

O'Reilly, C. A., III, & Tushman, M. L. (2004). The ambidextrous organization. *Harvard Business Review, 82*(4), 74–81.

Osterwalder, A., & Pigneur, Y. (2010). *Business model generation*. Wiley.

Parker, G., Van Alstyne, M., & Choudary, S. P. (2016). *Platform revolution*. W. W. Norton.

Teece, D. J. (1986). Profiting from technological innovation: Implications for integration, collaboration, licensing and public policy. *Research Policy, 15*(6), 285 305.

Tukker, A. (2004). Eight types of product–service system: Eight ways to sustainability? *Business Strategy and the Environment*, 13(4), 246–260.

United Nations. (2015). *Transforming our world: The 2030 agenda for sustainable development*. United Nations.

Chapter 14
Designing the Future

Abstract Returning to 3A with a systemic, evolutionary stance, we argue for artifacts as evolvable architectures (modularity, open interfaces, traceability), actors as human–AI constellations with participation and power designed in, and actions as instrumented, auditable, iterated interventions. We outline governance for learning at scale and ethical guardrails for AI-intensive systems. The chapter closes with practical principles for steering emergence—shaping futures that are innovative, accountable, and sustainable.

Design Must Evolve

Design does not merely react to the future; design helps make it. The systems now taking shape—cyber–physical–human, data-rich, and institutionally entangled—produce complex, unpredictable outcomes that no single artifact or team can control. Futures are always partly designed and partly evolved. The quality of our architectures, decisions, and collaborations will determine which evolutions take root—and, just as importantly, those futures will reshape the practice of design itself.

Small choices at one interface can cascade elsewhere—safety on roads, fairness in markets, and resilience in infrastructure. Meeting that reality demands higher order empathy and creativity aimed at human outcomes, not only at product specs. The core moves endure—empathy, ideation, prototyping, convergence—but their scope widens. Empathy stretches from users to citizens and communities. Ideation spans features, business models, and policies. Prototyping shifts from artifacts to sandboxes and staged rollouts. Convergence integrates desirability, feasibility, viability, legitimacy, and sustainability. Above all, architecture is destiny: structure—of products, processes, organizations, and ecosystems—governs behavior and must embed "ilities" (e.g., reliability, evolvability, sustainability) from the outset.

J. Luo, *Design Science*, Applied Innovation and Technology Management,
https://doi.org/10.1007/978-3-032-13353-3_14

Evolutionary Ecosystem Design Thinking

We design into moving systems. New value emerges as domains connect (e.g., mobility + energy + information); new risks emerge for the same reason (security, equity, accountability). Designers cannot optimize to a fixed end state; they must place good bets, set guardrails, and invite beneficial evolution. Practically, that means making dependency structure visible (with DSMs and change-propagation models), thinning and stabilizing crossing points, aligning organizational and inter-firm roles with real coupling, and versioning decisions so responsibilities and trade-offs remain traceable. The aim is not perfect control but resilient direction—enough structure for progress, enough openness for emergence.

AI as Amplifier—Inside Human-Led Governance

AI changes the feasible set. Foundation models offer broad knowledge and versatile reasoning; agentic systems orchestrate tools, tests, and documentation. Used well—grounded, verified, and governed—AI widens search (divergence), tightens loops (convergence), and lifts the attainable frontier of originality and performance. As AI takes on a more active role in analysis, generation, and orchestration, human leadership must strengthen and systematize: leaders define goals, roles, guardrails, and escalation paths that make hybrid human–AI workflows reliable, contestable, and accountable. In this mode, AI is a disciplined amplifier—not an oracle—operating inside well-architected processes.

Systems Leadership—Now with AI in the Loop

Systems thinking helps designers see cross-boundary feedbacks and second-order effects. Systems leadership mobilizes the coalitions that can act on those insights and govern complex, hybrid workflows. Leaders convene diverse actors, translate between technical and civic languages, and hold space for principled trade-offs. They set shared outcomes and transparent metrics, publish known limitations, embed verification and red-team rituals in the cadence, and learn in public through pilots and staged rollouts. With that discipline, designing the future becomes a human-led, hybrid-intelligence enterprise rather than a patchwork of local optimizations.

The Future of Design Is Hybrid Intelligence

Because the landscape is changing, design itself must evolve around teams of people and AI models working together—hybrid intelligence:

- From artifact craft to system stewardship. Designers spend more time shaping architectures—product, process, organization, ecosystem—where long-run behavior lives, and less time polishing isolated features.
- From tools to orchestrated toolchains. Workflows couple requirements, AI models, CAD/code, simulators, and data with provenance and policy layers; the design record becomes executable and auditable.
- From individual genius to hybrid intelligence. Humans pose questions, set constraints, interpret evidence, make value trade-offs, and decide when to stop; AI explores, proposes, tests, and documents—under guardrails that keep accountability legible.
- From static briefs to living contracts. Interfaces and policies are versioned; decisions are designed for reversibility where possible; change-propagation analysis guides what to freeze, where to flex, and how to roll updates safely.
- From stated ethics to operational responsibility. Fairness, safety, privacy, and sustainability move from statements to mechanisms—constraints, monitors, escalation paths—in the stack.
- From curricula to capabilities. Education leans into systems thinking, AI/data literacy, verification, and public reasoning—so designers can steer hybrid workflows, govern evidence, and keep values in the loop.

The through line is clear: rising complexity and deeper AI participation do not diminish the need for human leadership—they raise the bar. The design practices that thrive will treat hybrid intelligence as a core design material and systems leadership as a core capability, pairing expansive creativity with disciplined governance. The question, then, is how to make that stance operational from week to week and release to release.

Revisiting Artifact–Actor–Action

In Chap. 1 we framed design as Artifact–Actor–Action. Seen from the future, each is a trajectory under technical, economic, social, and ecological selection. Artifacts evolve from products to platforms to ecosystems; Actors expand from individual users to multi-stakeholder constellations—including organizations, communities, and increasingly AI agents; Actions shift from one-off launches to continuous, instrumented interventions that learn and adapt. We design into moving systems, and what we design in turn reshapes the systems that select and scale it.

A systemic lens widens the unit of design. For Artifacts, interfaces, standards, and data provenance matter as much as form and performance. Architecture is destiny because structure governs behavior across releases and partners. For Actors, value and risk distribute across networks—customers, citizens, frontline workers, regulators, suppliers, and algorithms. So, inclusion, incentives, and accountability are design variables, not afterthoughts. For Actions, deployments become coupled experiments (plan → release → measure → learn → update), with guardrails—risk tiers, reversible-first choices, red-team rituals—keeping speed aligned with responsibility. This is how design steers emergence without pretending to control it.

Accordingly, artifacts are conceived as evolvable architectures—modular, open, and traceable. Actors are enabled by participation and power by design—clear roles, aligned incentives, recourse, and explicit recognition of human–AI joint agency. Actions function as iterated trials—instrumented with telemetry, grounded in provenance from data to decision, and safeguarded by audits that scale with impact. Reconnecting 3A in this way keeps the discipline future-ready: we steer what changes, stabilize what matters, and keep consequences visible as ecosystems evolve.

A Practical Stance for Designing Futures

Designing futures benefits from principles that are explicit enough to guide trade-offs and light-weight enough to use under pressure. The moves below turn intent into habit: they keep values computable, architectures legible, ecosystems coordinated, AI accountable, and leadership visible—so progress remains both fast and responsible.

- Start from values and "ilities." Treat safety, dignity, equity, reliability, evolvability, and sustainability as first-class, computable requirements alongside cost and performance. Write them into objectives and tests, not just statements; make them traceable from requirement to verification.
- Architect for legibility and evolution. Map dependencies (e.g., with DSMs and change-propagation views), stabilize interfaces, and separate capability (what the system can do) from policy (what it may do here and now). Version decisions and contracts so responsibilities and trade-offs remain auditable as conditions change.
- Design the ecosystem, not just the artifact. Decide deliberately what to open to attract complements and what to keep integral for safety or differentiation. Align release cadences, certification, and accountability across partners so cooperation scales without constant renegotiation.
- Use AI as a disciplined amplifier. Ground outputs in trusted corpora and simulators; wrap interactions with verification harnesses; log lineage for reproducibility; and keep humans in the loop for goals, exceptions, and value judgments. Let AI widen search and tighten loops—without relaxing governance.
- Lead as you design. Convene stakeholders early, make trade-offs explicit and contestable, publish known limitations, and build audits and pilots into the product itself. Measure learning, not just launch, so evidence compounds and trust is continually earned.

Outlook

The future will not arrive as a blank brief, nor hinge on a single invention. It will emerge from linked choices about architectures, interfaces, incentives, and norms—some ours, some others', many interacting. Designers can tilt that emergence toward human flourishing by coupling creativity with structure and insight with systems leadership. If the practice evolves—toward human-led hybrid intelligence and rigorous stewardship of complex systems—we can help shape futures that are not only technologically advanced, but also legible, just, and sustainable.

FSC
www.fsc.org
MIX
Papier aus verantwortungsvollen Quellen
Paper from responsible sources
FSC® C105338

If you have any concerns about our products,
you can contact us on
ProductSafety@springernature.com

In case Publisher is established outside the EU,
the EU authorized representative is:
Springer Nature Customer Service Center GmbH
Europaplatz 3, 69115 Heidelberg, Germany

Printed by Libri Plureos GmbH
in Hamburg, Germany